DRAWING
CONCEPTS

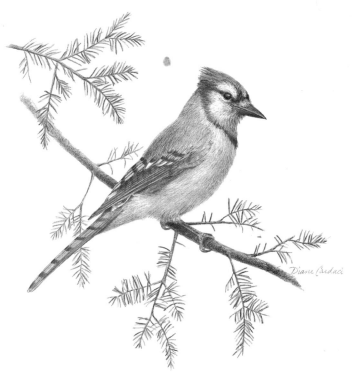

With Diane Cardaci, Ken Goldman, William F. Powell, and Carol Rosinski

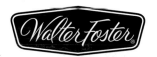

www.walterfoster.com

This book has been produced to aid the aspiring artist. Reproduction of work for study or finished art is permissible. Any art produced or photomechanically reproduced from this publication for commercial purposes is forbidden without written consent from the publisher, Walter Foster Publishing, Inc.

Project Editor: Elizabeth T. Gilbert • Designed by Shelley Baugh • Production Design by Debbie Aiken

3 5 7 9 10 8 6 4 2

CONTENTS

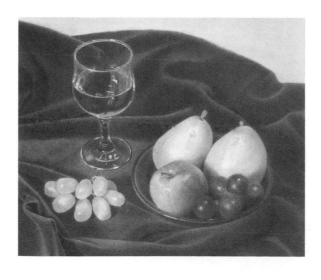

TOOLS AND MATERIALS

The artist's greatest tool is the imagination. But before we start exercising this asset, it's important to get to know the range of tools that can act as extensions of your imagination, allowing you to transfer what's in your head to your drawing surface. All you really need to start are a pencil, eraser, and paper. But there are a few other items that will come in handy as well—and they're all explained here.

Pencils

Artist's pencils (A) contain a graphite center ("lead") and are sorted by hardness ("grades"), from very soft (labeled 9B) to very hard (labeled 9H). You don't need a pencil of every grade when you first begin drawing; a good starting collection for this book is 6B, 4B, 2B, HB, B, 2H, 4H, and 6H. Keep in mind that pencil hardness is not standardized, so one brand's 2H pencil might be the same as another brand's B. For this reason, your first group of pencils should be of the same brand. An alternative to wooden pencils are lead holders (B). Usually made of metal and plastic, *lead holders* resemble pencils but are actually hollow, reusable holders for individual leads. Purchased separately, the lead refills are placed in the holder, which has a clutch action near the tip to hold the lead tightly; when you press the opposite end, the tip releases, letting out as much lead as you need. Leads are about 5" long and 2mm in diameter; they usually are sold in packages of a dozen of one grade. Although lead holders are convenient and easy to use, beginners usually start with the more economical wooden pencils.

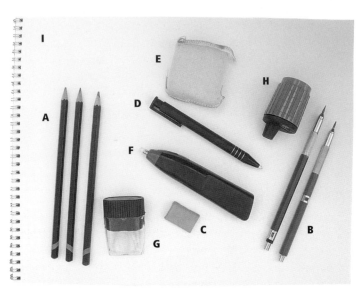

Purchasing the Essentials Your local arts and crafts store is sure to carry the basic items shown above. Keep in mind that it's best to purchase the highest quality materials you can afford, as these produce the best results.

Erasers

There are three basic types of erasers for use in pencil drawing: kneaded (C), stick (D), and pillow (E). *Kneaded* erasers are very soft and can be molded into different shapes. *Stick* erasers come in pen-shaped holders and easily can be carved into a point using a craft knife or razor blade. *Pillow* erasers are made of a loosely woven cloth filled with loose erasing material, allowing you to clean up smudges and accidental marks on large areas.

Sharpeners

If you are using wooden pencils, a simple hand-held sharpener (G) that catches the shavings is a good choice. Electric sharpeners also are great, as they quickly produce a very sharp tip. If you are using lead holders, be sure to buy the appropriate sharpener for your brand (H).

Brushes

Brushes aren't usually thought of as a drawing tool, but they can be extremely useful for creating smooth blends and gradations and for applying graphite dust directly to the drawing surface. You can use any flat, soft-bristle paintbrush for this method. Small brushes with short bristles allow for more accuracy, so you may have to trim the bristles to the desired length with a small pair of sharp scissors.

Papers

For practice sketches, purchase a medium-weight (50- to 60-lb) paper pad, which is bound with tape or a wire spiral (I). For more finished drawings, buy a heavy-weight paper (about 70- to 80-lb). Most paper is made from cotton fibers (rag) and/or wood pulp, but you also can buy recycled papers. Wood pulp papers are the least expensive and are great for beginners. Cotton fiber papers are more expensive but also are more durable. Paper texture (the "tooth") also varies: *Plate* or *hot-press* paper is smooth and allows for softer blends and smooth shading, whereas *vellum* or *cold-press* paper is rough and allows for strokes with more texture.

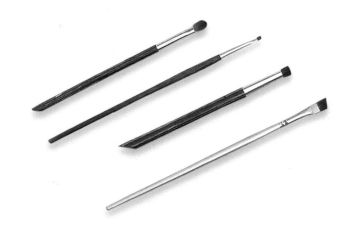

Trimming Bristles When trimming the bristles of a paintbrush, cut the bristles at a slight angle (you'll be holding the brush at an angle to the paper). The trimmed brush has stiffer bristles that give you much more control when working with graphite.

Extras

The materials on these pages are only the basics—there are many other items (some of which are shown at right) that may be of assistance as you draw. A *blow bulb* comes in handy for blowing away loose graphite dust and eraser crumbs without disturbing the drawing beneath (A). A small craft knife is an ideal tool for shaping erasers (B). A *blending stump*—soft paper packed into the shape of a slim cylinder—is used for smearing and blending (C). Emery boards can sharpen pencils and help you create piles of loose graphite (D). *Pencil extenders* add length to your short pencils so you can grip them properly (E). And *spray fixative* prevents your finished piece from smudging (F). It's also a good idea to purchase a plastic toolbox with a handle to store your tools between drawing sessions.

Setting Up Your Workspace

Choose your workspace to match your style. Some people like to stand to allow free arm movement; others prefer to sit at a table for more precise work. Wherever you do your drawing, you will need good lighting: a floor lamp, desk light, or clamp-on light. As an artist, you may prefer to use a "natural" or "daylight" bulb, which mimics sunlight and is easy on your eye. To avoid blocking the light with your body or hand—if you're right-handed—place the light to your left and above your work; left-handed artists, put your lamp to the right and above.

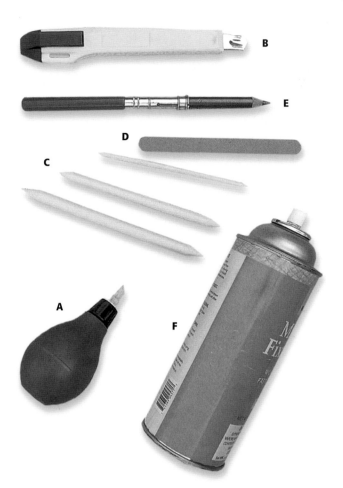

▲ **Gathering Additional Items** Most of the items pictured above can be found at your local arts and crafts store. Others, such as tissues and cotton swabs, you may already have in your kitchen or bathroom!

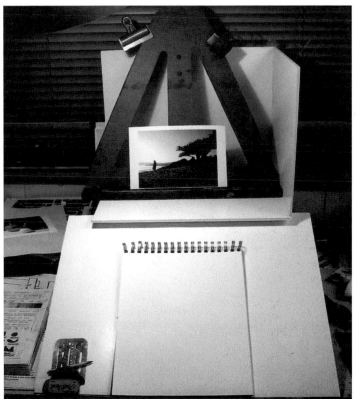

◄ **Ken Goldman's Work Station** Artist Ken Goldman finds it convenient to include a *still life box* in his work area. "My work station functions well for working with both photos and actual objects. When creating a still life, I arrange my objects in a still life box. This box serves as a 'stage' on which I can produce various effects with lighting and backdrops (see page 27). I constructed the still life box shown in the photo from three pieces of foam core (two 12" x 16" rectangles for one side and the base, plus one 12" x 12" square for the remaining side), held together with clear packing tape. I set the still life box on a sturdy box against which I have leaned a foam core drawing board, placing everything at a comfortable height for me to sit and work. To draw from a photo, I simply place a table easel in the still life box. The clips on the easel are useful for raising a small image closer to eye level."

HANDLING THE PENCIL

You can create an incredible variety of effects with a pencil. By using various hand positions, you can produce a world of different lines and strokes. If you vary the way you hold your pencil, the mark the pencil makes changes. It's just as important to notice your pencil point. The point is every bit as essential as the type of lead in the pencil. Experiment with different hand positions and pencil points to see what your pencil can do!

There are two main hand positions for drawing. The writing position is good for very detailed

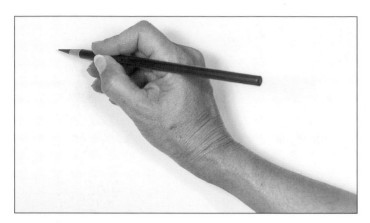

Using the Writing Position The writing position is exactly what it sounds like! Hold the pencil as you normally do while writing. Most of your detail work will be done this way, using the point of the pencil.

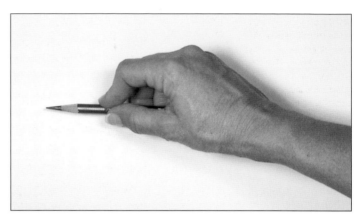

Using the Underhand Position Pick up the pencil with your hand over it, holding the pencil between the thumb and index finger; the remaining fingers can rest alongside the pencil. You can create beautiful shading effects from this position.

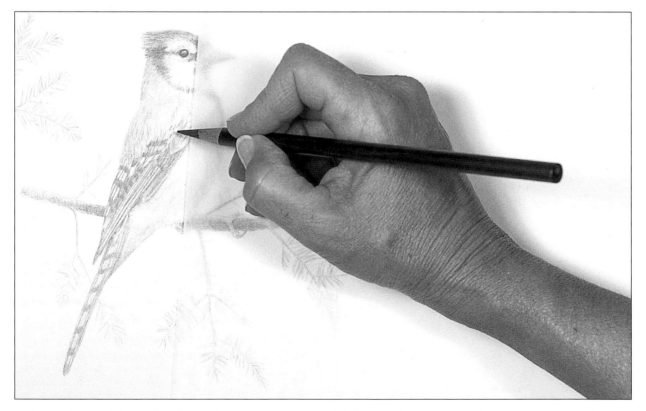

Protecting Your Art It's a good idea to use a piece of tracing paper as a barrier between your hand and your drawing. The tracing paper not only prevents you from smudging your drawing, but it also keep oils from your skin from damaging the art.

PRACTICING LINES

When drawing lines, it is not necessary to always use a sharp point. In fact, sometimes a blunt point may create a more desirable effect. When using larger lead diameters, the effect of a blunt point is even more evident. Play around with your pencils to familiarize yourself with the different types of lines they can create. Make every kind of stroke you can think of, using both a sharp point and a blunt point. Practice the strokes below to help you loosen up.

As you experiment, you will find that some of your doodles will bring to mind certain imagery or textures. For example, little Vs may bring birds to mind, or wavy lines might suggest water.

Drawing with a Sharp Point
First draw a series of parallel lines. Try them vertically; then angle them. Make some of them curved, trying both short and long strokes. Then try some wavy lines at an angle and some with short, vertical strokes. You may also want to try making a spiral and then try grouping short, curved lines together. Then practice varying the weight of the line as you draw.

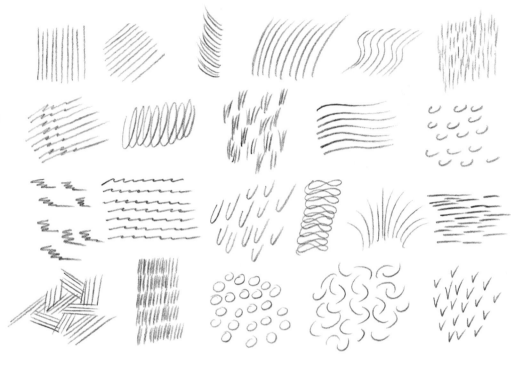

Drawing with a Blunt Point
It is good to take the same exercises and try them with a blunt point. Even if you use the same hand positions and strokes, the results will be different when you switch pencils. Take a look at the examples at right. Diane Cardaci drew the same shapes with both pencils, but the blunt pencil produced different images. Her favorite blunt-point tool is a 6B large-diameter lead that she uses with a lead holder.

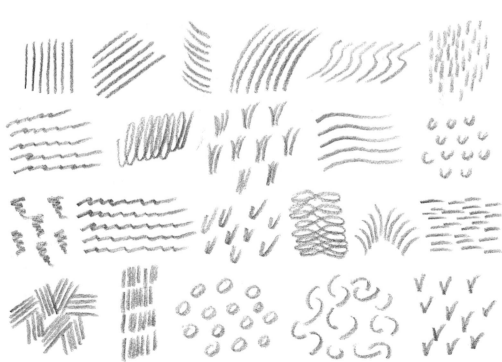

SHADING TECHNIQUES

As you'll see in Chapter 1, value is essential in suggesting the form, or three-dimensional quality, of a subject. There are many ways to apply and manipulate graphite on your paper to create a range of values, but *how* you apply the graphite is what determines the texture of the subject. Explore the techniques on the following pages so that you can learn a variety of shading styles and pair the appropriate technique with a subject.

Hatching and Crosshatching

The most direct way to lay down a layer of graphite to create a darker value is by simple *hatching,* which is a series of parallel strokes. If you squint your eyes and look at a hatched area, the lines seem to mix together to form a value that is darker than the paper yet lighter than the actual lines of graphite. The closer you place the parallel strokes, the darker the value.

Overlapping Lines A simple way to create a darker value using hatching (upper left) is by adding the same pattern of lines perpendicular to the first layer of hatching (lower right). This is called "crosshatching." Cross-hatching is a quick, all-purpose way to add value and texture to a drawing.

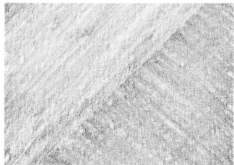

Using the Side of the Pencil Create a softer look by hatching with the side of your pencil (upper left). Again, you can darken an area more by cross-hatching over it (lower right). This type of hatching might be a good choice if you are drawing a lightly textured cloth or a field of weeds.

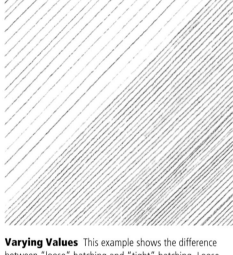

Varying Values This example shows the difference between "loose" hatching and "tight" hatching. Loose hatching, with the lines spread far apart (upper left), is best for areas of light value; the tighter, or closer, the hatch strokes, the darker the area will be (lower right).

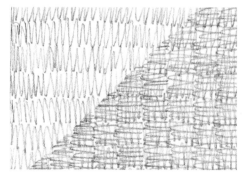

Making Scribbles If you make an even, but rough-textured, scribble hatch (upper left) and then crosshatch (lower right), you can create a seamlike quality that might be used to draw loosely woven fabric, mesh, or basketry.

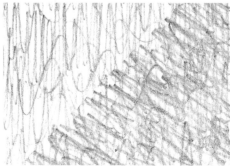

Combining Methods You can create hatching with any type of line. I made this hatch and crosshatch with a loose, uneven scribble movement. It yields an interesting texture that would be perfect for rendering distant foliage.

Applying Smooth Hatching

Although hatching with bold, rough strokes is great for quickly identifying areas of shading in a sketch, applying finely hatched lines yields a more finished look. This technique is called "smooth hatching." Smooth hatching takes a bit of practice to master, but it is essential for creating gradations that suggest evenness of texture, curvature, and form. Like so much of drawing, your ability to make a smooth hatch will improve as you gain more control over your tools. Follow the exercises at the top of the next page to practice the subtlety of pencil pressure associated with smooth hatching.

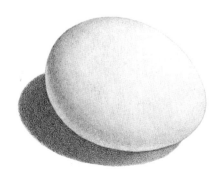

Mastering Smooth Hatching After some practice, you will be able to create a tight hatch that needs no further smoothing or blending with stumps or brushes, as demonstrated with this egg.

Exercise One Using medium pressure, draw a square and divide it in half diagonally. In the lower right corner, use a sharp B lead and minimal pressure to create a light hatch. Then create a dark hatch in the opposite corner using heavier pressure. Continue hatching from the dark area toward the centerline, using increasingly less pressure as you reach the middle. Develop the gradation even more by filling in areas between the hatch marks.

Exercise Two Now execute a similar smooth hatching, this time concentrating on extending the darker value past the diagonal halfway mark. For this exercise, experiment with a softer grade of pencil to suit the darker value. For example, try a 4B within the dark half and gradate to a B for the lighter side. The more you stroke over the sample (avoiding heavy pressure that may damage the paper's surface), the smoother the hatch will become.

Understanding the Properties of Pencils

Two important factors to consider when creating a value with graphite are the degree of hardness of the pencil and the sharpness of the tip. It's much easier to create a dark value with a soft pencil than with a hard one, and the softer pencil will leave a rougher-looking texture when stroked over the grain of the paper. The diverse looks created by different grades of lead can be used to mimic textures of objects in your drawings. Also try creating samples with both sharpened and dull pencil points; you'll see that the sharper the pencil, the darker your value will be, even when you're using the same amount of pressure.

Using Sharp and Dull Points
Sharpen a B pencil to a very fine point and fill a box using medium pressure (above, top left). As your pencil dulls, create another box using the same pressure (above, top right). You will see that the sharpness of the lead creates different values and textures. I used a 2B pencil for the bottom row, also using sharp, then dull, points.

Effecting Value Through Grade Each of these graduated samples is made with a different grade of lead (from left to right): 4H, 2H, B, 2B, and 4B.

Changing Grades to Achieve a Dark Value

Although it's easier to create a dark value with a soft lead than with a hard lead, you'll find that the soft lead actually skips over parts of the paper, leaving behind little white spots that dilute the value. It's tempting to just press harder with the pencil to achieve a dark value, but this only flattens the grain of the paper, creating an especially shiny and distracting spot on your drawing. To create a very dark value without flattening the grain of your paper, first go over the area several times with a very sharp, soft lead, using light to medium pressure. Follow this with a slightly harder, sharp lead. The harder lead pushes the previously applied, softer graphite into the grain of the paper that was skipped over before, so the entire area is coated—there won't be any white areas or shiny spots.

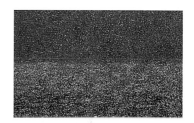

Layering First shade with a soft lead (7B). Then use a slightly harder lead (4B) to go over the top half using the same pressure. Compare the two areas and notice the effect of the hard lead on the value.

Hard over Soft In this example, I applied 7B first in the top two thirds, followed by 2H in the bottom two thirds. The center area of overlap shows how hard lead applied over soft lead darkens the value.

Soft over Hard Here I applied 2H first in the bottom two thirds, followed by 7B in the top two thirds. The center area of overlap shows how soft lead doesn't stick on surfaces coated with hard lead.

DRAWING WHAT YOU SEE

Most people are accustomed to drawing what they *think* they see, which is simply the *idea* of the object in our minds. Our brains aren't accustomed to recording detailed observations, so we must concentrate on retaining and recalling details for our drawings. Practice drawing what you see.

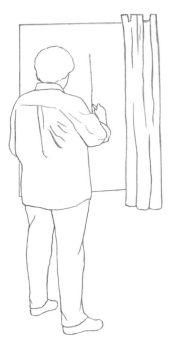

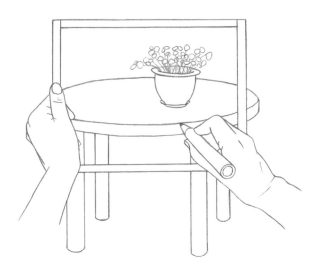

Portable Window Create a portable window from a piece of rigid acrylic, which is available at your local hardware store. Try the same window outline exercise indoors; it will help you understand how to reproduce the challenging angles and curves of your subject.

Window Outline Exercise To train your eye and brain to observe, stand or sit in front of a window and trace the outline of a tree or car onto the glass with an erasable marker. If you move your head, your line will no longer correspond accurately with the subject, so try to keep it still.

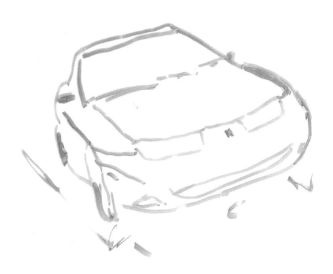

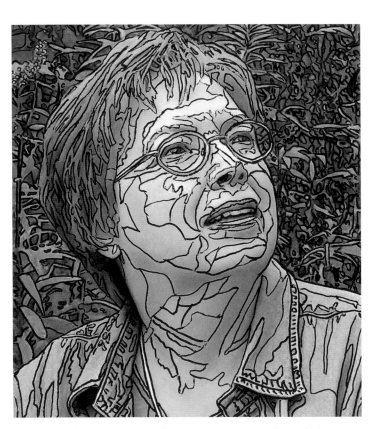

Foreshortening in a Window Drawing *Foreshortening*—when an object is angled toward the viewer—causes the closest parts of an object to appear much larger than parts that are farther away. This can be a difficult concept to master, but a window drawing, shown above, simplifies this process.

Looking at Photos Another beneficial way to observe impartially is to find an interesting photo in a magazine. Outline all the shapes and values you see with a pen. Take your time and indicate even the smallest change in value.

Measuring with a Pencil

Drawing the correct *proportions*—the size relationships between different parts of an object—is easier if you learn to take measurements directly from your subject and then transfer those to your paper. You can measure your subject with just about anything (for example, your thumb). Using a pencil is a very easy and accurate way to take measurements, as shown below.

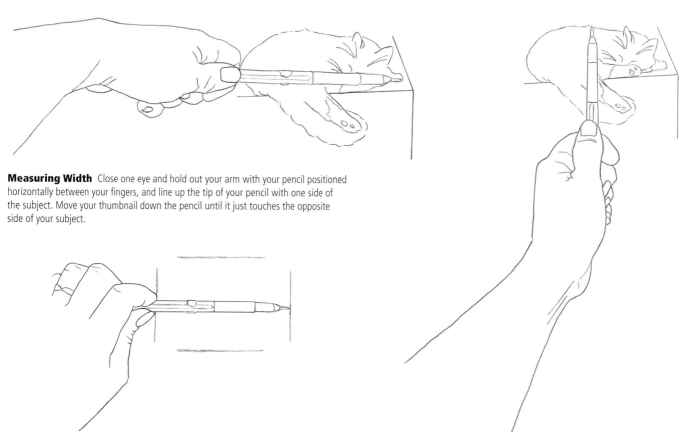

Measuring Width Close one eye and hold out your arm with your pencil positioned horizontally between your fingers, and line up the tip of your pencil with one side of the subject. Move your thumbnail down the pencil until it just touches the opposite side of your subject.

Transferring Measurements Mark the length of your pencil measurements on your paper. If you want to enlarge the subject, multiply each measurement by two or three. If you extend the initial markings to this new measurement, you can form a box around your subject that will work like a grid to help you draw your subject using correct proportions.

Measuring Height Using the same procedure, measure the distance between the highest and lowest points of your subject.

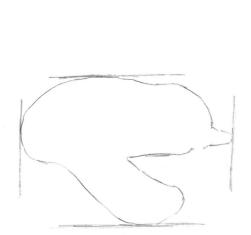

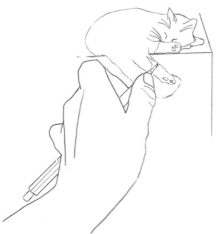

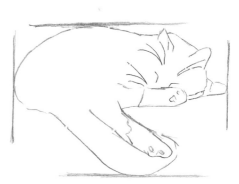

Adding Up the Numbers After you've created the basic rectangle, using the tallest and widest measurements of the subject, sketch the cat's general shape within the rectangle. Keep the shape simple and add details later.

Mapping Out Elements As long as you stay in the same position with your arm extended at full length, you can take additional measurements, such as the cat's foot here, which will be in proportion to the rest of the body.

Correcting Calculations While progressing from a basic shape to a gradually more detailed outline drawing, take measurements before applying any marks to keep your drawing in proportion.

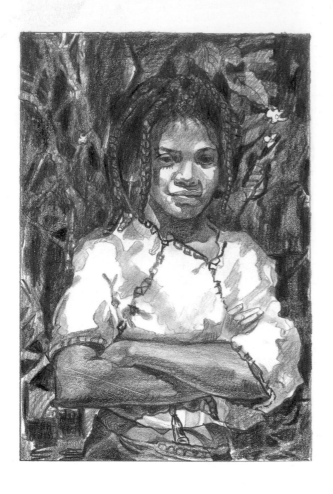

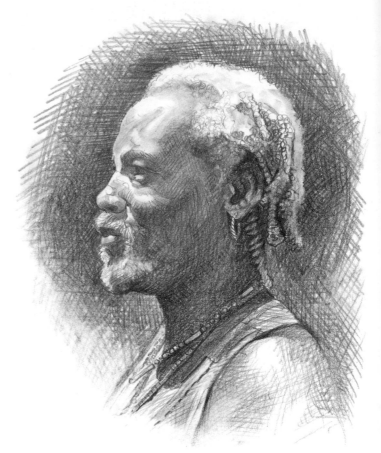

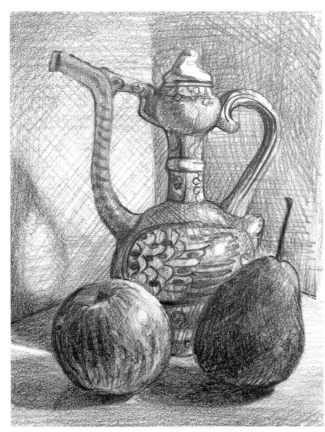

CHAPTER 1

UNDERSTANDING VALUES

with Ken Goldman

This is not just a "how-to" chapter; it is a "how-to-see-and-do" chapter. When seeing and drawing shapes and their values—lightness or darkness—you are not drawing "things." Rather, you are creating areas of value as various shapes; those shapes become recognizable only when they are drawn accurately in combination with other shapes. This is an effective, time-tested approach, but its application requires some rethinking of childhood drawing preconceptions, as well as discipline in seeing and drawing differently.

The exercises in this chapter will take you through a step-by-step process of seeing shapes, identifying their light and dark values, and fitting the pieces together to form recognizable images. By seeing and drawing objectively, rather than by thoughtlessly copying, you will be able to create a realistic subject.

—Ken Goldman

About Ken Goldman

Ken Goldman is a popular instructor at the Athenaeum School of the Arts in La Jolla, California, where he teaches portraiture, artistic anatomy, and landscape painting classes. Ken received his training in New York at the Art Students League, National Academy of Design, and New York Studio School. A recipient of numerous awards, Ken has exhibited widely in group shows and in more than 30 one-man shows in the United States, Mexico, and Europe. His artwork is featured in the permanent collections of several major museums. Ken lives in San Diego, California, with his artist-wife Stephanie Goldman.

BASIC STROKES

The moment your pencil touches paper, you have made a statement. Value, line, texture, and shape are elements that you, the artist, can use to convey ideas. In this drawing, I use various strokes to depict a rabbit sitting alertly in a field. In artistic terms, the recognizable shape is a rabbit, surrounded by various combinations of textures, values, and lines that tell us about the field. Practice these strokes and note how and where they are used throughout this chapter.

Adding Texture Note the effect created in the drawing by each basic stroke shown here. Experiment with a blending stump to see which additional textures you can create.

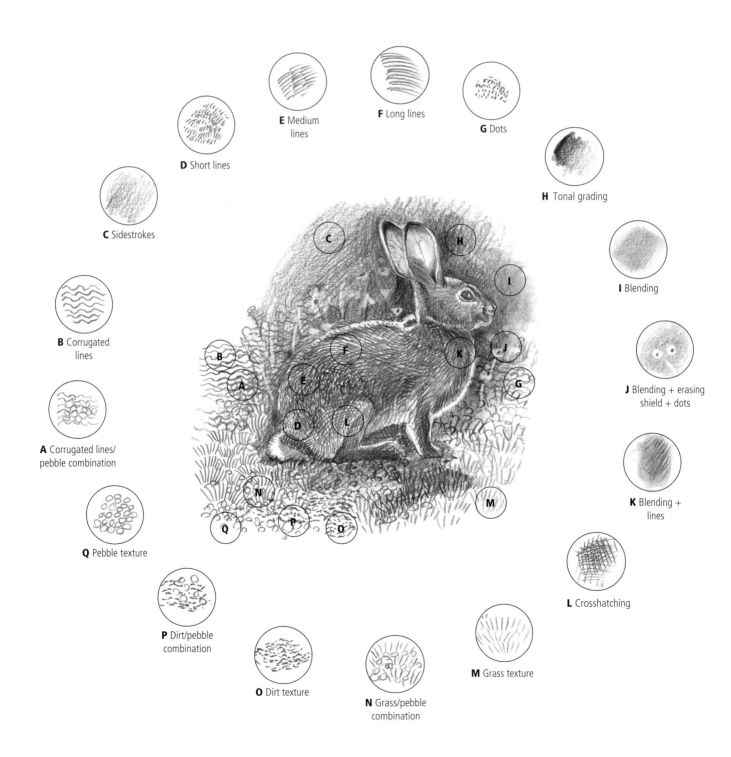

E Medium lines

F Long lines

G Dots

D Short lines

H Tonal grading

C Sidestrokes

I Blending

B Corrugated lines

J Blending + erasing shield + dots

A Corrugated lines/ pebble combination

K Blending + lines

Q Pebble texture

L Crosshatching

P Dirt/pebble combination

M Grass texture

O Dirt texture

N Grass/pebble combination

UNDERSTANDING VALUE AND SHAPE

Value is defined as the relative lightness or darkness of a color or of black. In nature, values have infinite *gradations,* or degrees. The shapes that we see are a result of these changes in value. Because artists cannot visually comprehend such unlimited subtleties, they reduce nature's vast scale into values that they easily can see. Many artists use a scale of nine values ranging from black through gray to white. I often use only five: highlight, light, medium, dark, and low dark.

Establishing a Value Scale

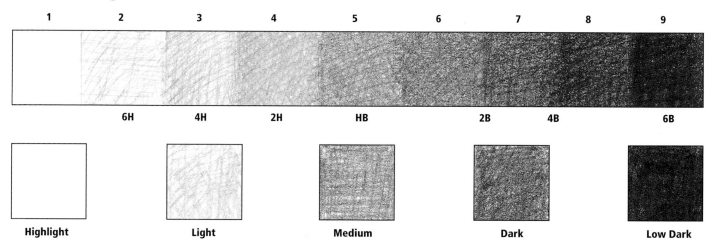

| Highlight | Light | Medium | Dark | Low Dark |

Rendering Values The nine-value scale shows the transition from white through gray to black. The numbers and letters underneath the scale show you which pencils I use for each value. The 6H is the hardest lead and barely makes a mark; it works well for delicate shading, such as value 2. The 4H is slightly softer and, depending on how much pressure you apply, will create values 2, 3, and 4. The 2H is good for light lay-ins; it works well for value 4, and its soft lead will not leave grooves in fragile paper. The HB is my favorite pencil for all-around drawing, and it's perfect for the middle-value 5. The 2B has a wide range: It represents values 6 and 7 on the scale. The 4B is a soft, dark pencil that corresponds to values 7 and 8 on the scale. The 6B is slightly darker than the 4B; it creates a velvety black corresponding with value 9, but it easily breaks when being sharpened.

Recognizing Shapes

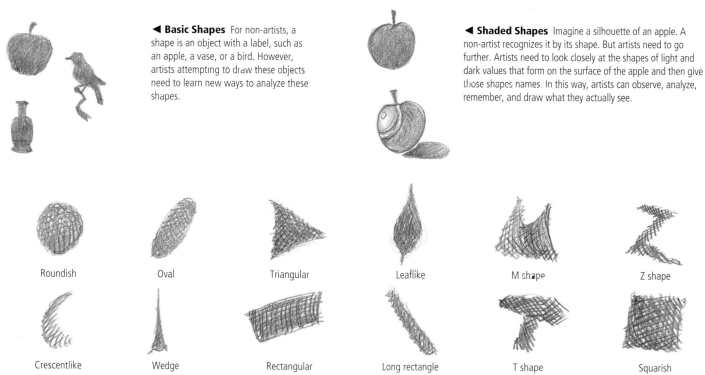

◄ **Basic Shapes** For non-artists, a shape is an object with a label, such as an apple, a vase, or a bird. However, artists attempting to draw these objects need to learn new ways to analyze these shapes.

◄ **Shaded Shapes** Imagine a silhouette of an apple. A non-artist recognizes it by its shape. But artists need to go further. Artists need to look closely at the shapes of light and dark values that form on the surface of the apple and then give those shapes names. In this way, artists can observe, analyze, remember, and draw what they actually see.

| Roundish | Oval | Triangular | Leaflike | M shape | Z shape |
| Crescentlike | Wedge | Rectangular | Long rectangle | T shape | Squarish |

Abstract Shapes These are random examples of shapes you may see in various objects and suggestions for names you can use to help you remember what shapes you intend to draw. By learning to carefully place shapes you actually see, you will gain the type of objectivity that is necessary to draw anything in front of you.

SEEING VALUES

There is a saying among artists: "Color gets all the attention while value does all the work." Whether you draw an object with a two-, five-, or nine-value scale, it is value, not color, that is mainly responsible for the visual strength of the image. With practice, you can train yourself to view objects and scenes in terms of their values.

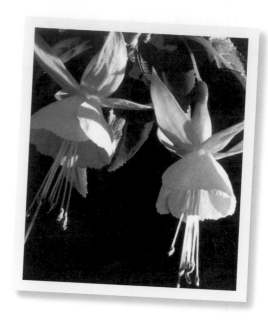

▶ **Translating Color to Value** This photo of fuchsia was shot in brilliant color. But the range of values is what gives the image strength in black-and-white.

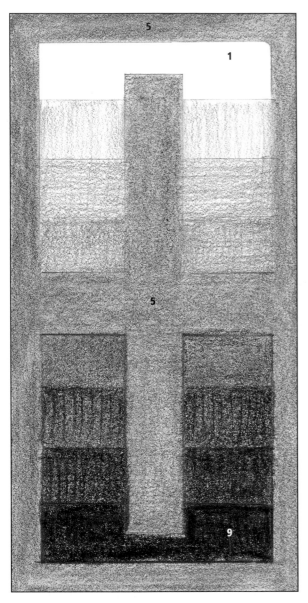

▲ **Recognizing Contrasts** An artist can achieve a wide range of contrasts with the help of *simultaneous contrast*—the illusion that a middle-value (5) gray appears darker when surrounded by white (1) and lighter when surrounded by black (9). (The middle-value gray column and border in this image actually have the same value from top to bottom and all around.)

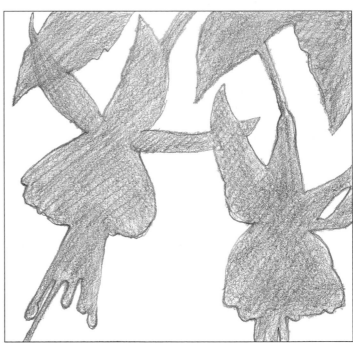

▲ **Simplifying Values** The first stage in seeing values is to simplify. Two values (white and a middle-value 5 gray) are perfectly adequate to convey the idea of this fuchsia. Note how the light and dark areas of the silhouettes resemble certain shapes on page 15.

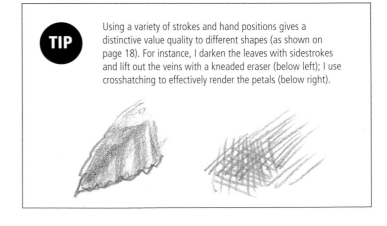

TIP Using a variety of strokes and hand positions gives a distinctive value quality to different shapes (as shown on page 18). For instance, I darken the leaves with sidestrokes and lift out the veins with a kneaded eraser (below left); I use crosshatching to effectively render the petals (below right).

Using Lines as a Shorthand for Value

Lines do not exist in nature, but they certainly exist in my drawings! I use lines as a shorthand method for transferring nature's three-dimensional world of light and dark onto my two-dimensional paper.

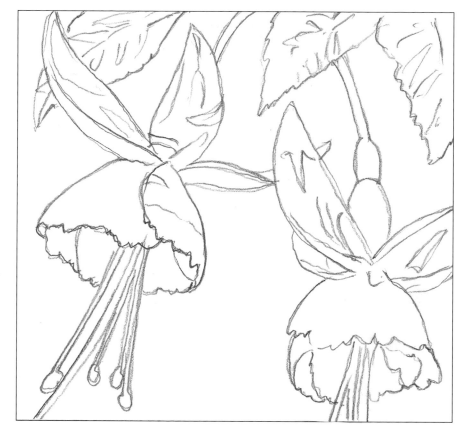

Representing Shapes with Lines The second stage in learning to see values is to find and draw the shapes within the overall form. Compare the flat, outlined silhouette on the opposite page with this line drawing. Instead of having a middle value, I add internal lines that break up the large main shape of each flower into smaller shapes, creating a linear sense of three dimensions and overlapping.

Combining Value and Line This drawing represents the third stage in seeing values. It combines the two values of the first stage with some of the lines from the second stage to further divide the shapes into smaller areas. Look back at page 15 and see how many shapes you can identify in the line drawing above. Next, look at the photograph on page 16. Compared with the photo's complexity of small veins, frills, and details, it's much simpler to begin a drawing with large, simple shapes like these.

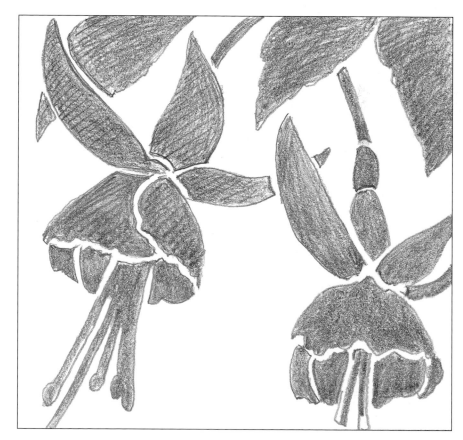

Introducing a Third Value

As I begin to render additional details to the shapes of light and shadow, I add a third value. This new, slightly lighter value allows me to incorporate the transitional subtleties that help give the fuchsia a sense of volume. Crosshatching and sidestrokes are two of my favorite methods for building up lights and darks. Try some of the strokes and textures shown on page 14 to see the effects you can create.

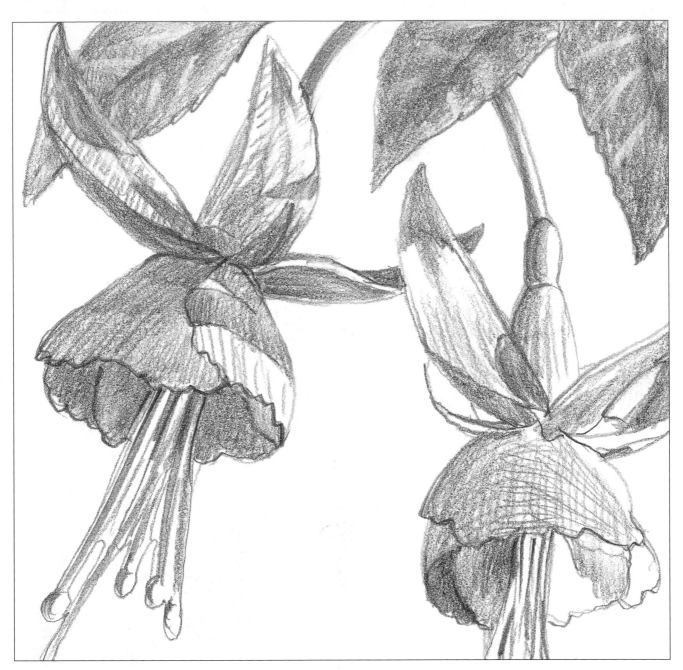

Creating Transitions Through the addition of a third middle value, the image begins to assume depth and volume. Because there are no areas darker than value 4, I can use an HB pencil for the whole drawing. The HB pencil is soft enough to make darks but also hard enough to render delicate lights, such as the outer petal of the left-hand flower and the inside petal of the right-hand flower.

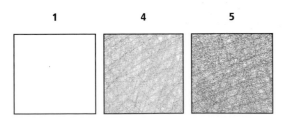

Adding a Lighter Middle Value For this version of my drawing, I add value 4, one step lighter than the middle-value 5 used in the earlier drawings.

18

Creating Drama with Additional Values

Compare the final drawing on this page with the three-value drawing on the opposite page. By adjusting the middle values to 3 and 6 and using black (9), I add both contrast and transition, bringing this version closer to the actual photo. This is an important point: How much should an artist deviate from a reference? The answer is that it depends on what degree of "finish" an artist prefers. Some artists like to copy a photo just as it is, and that's fine. The main difference between a photographic, realistic interpretation and the drawing on this page is that a super-realist will use the full value scale with its subtle gradations, whereas a drawing like this one uses only four values, resulting in less subtlety but more drama.

1	3	6	9

Adding Contrast The four values used for the final drawing are 1, 3, 6, and 9.

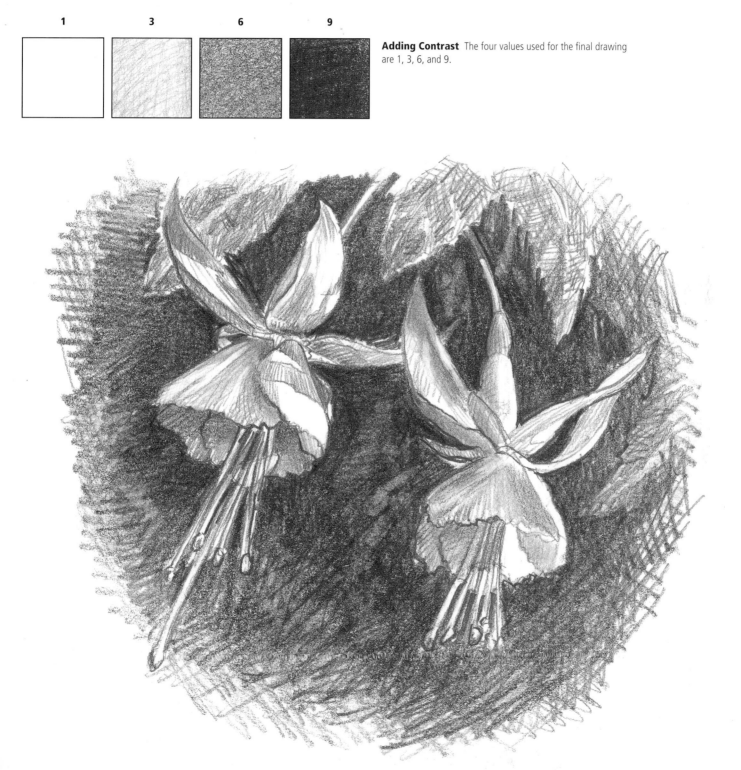

Interpreting the Subject Although the values in this drawing are similar to those in the photo, my use of looser, cross-hatched strokes makes this rendering more of an artistic interpretation than a strict copy.

PLACING SHAPES ACCURATELY

Knowing that drawing is a matter of seeing forms as shapes and values rather than preconceived objects is one thing; the next question is, "How do I find correct proportions and place those shapes accurately?" In addition to measuring (as shown on page 11), I use two techniques: seeing negative shapes, and drawing upside down.

Focusing on Negative Shapes

A non-artist can enjoy the graceful "positive shape" of this beautiful cypress tree and go no further. But an artist needs to see and be aware of the space *around* the cypress—the *negative shape*—in order to draw its outer shape. When I begin a drawing, I use negative shapes in conjunction with measurement. Before evaluating the negative shapes, I look for common measurements and make light construction lines.

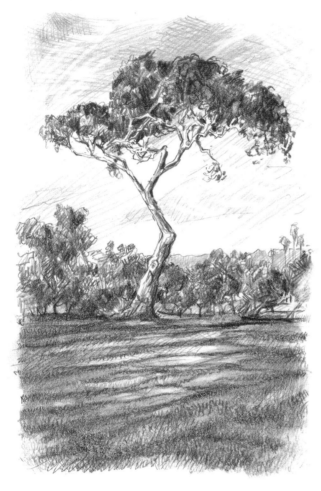

Measuring with the Eye Note that the overall height of the tree is exactly the same as the width of its canopy. This will help you draw the correct proportions when transferring the tree.

▶ **Creating Atmosphere** These are the values I used for this drawing: 1, 3, 6, and 8. There is no value 1 because any black in the distance would destroy the illusion of atmosphere and depth. (See page 38 for more on this.)

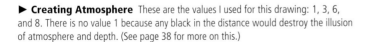

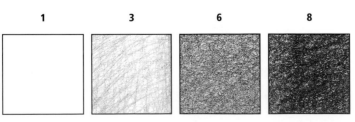

1	3	6	8

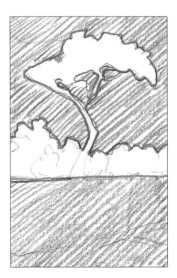

Understanding Freehand Drawing An exercise that will help you understand the essence of freehand drawing is to stand in one place, close one eye, and use a marker to trace the exact lines of your subject onto a rigid, transparent plastic sheet on which you have drawn grid lines. The verticals of the grid act as plumb lines, and the horizontals tell you how high or low one area is in relation to another. If you also draw a grid on your paper, transferring your tracing will be relatively easy. But freehand drawing implies the need to eventually transfer without using a grid. This is where the techniques of measuring and seeing negative shapes come in.

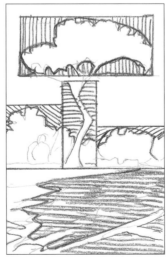

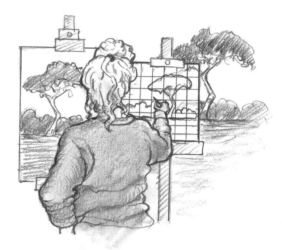

Cropping In After taking measurements to find the height and width of the cypress, I simulate a grid by lightly drawing rectangles and boxes around the canopy, trunk, and distant trees. "Cropping in" like this allows me to see positive-negative shape relationships better and helps me refine my drawing.

Interpreting Space The darkened sky and grass areas represent "negative" space around the trees; drawing the edge of these negative areas creates the "positive" shapes (trees). Conversely, drawing the edge of the positive trees creates the negative shapes (sky and grass).

Drawing Upside Down

Sometimes, when I am building up a drawing, I find that my preconceptions are so strong that it becomes almost impossible to continue drawing shapes and values objectively. The best solution I've found for regaining objectivity is to turn both the image I'm copying and my drawing paper upside down. Seeing the image upside down almost immediately negates the preconceptions of what your subject *should* look like, and you can begin to see the shapes objectively.

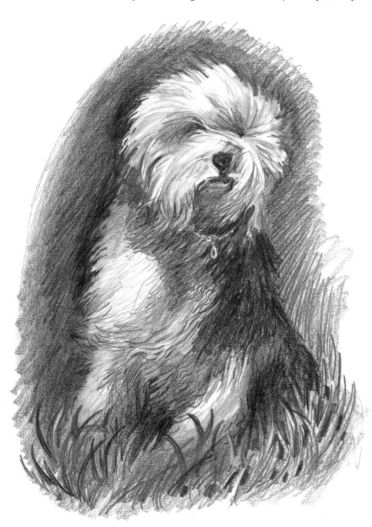

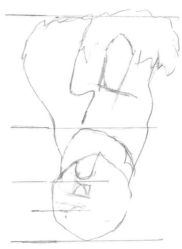

▲ **Step 1** After turning the photo of the dog upside down, I use an HB pencil to lightly sketch the dog on my drawing paper. I use shape identification, measurement, and negative shapes to capture the basic outline. The head is roundish, the neck crescentlike, the back a modified triangle, and the space between the legs a rectangle. I find the halfway mark at the top of the crescentlike shape; then I locate the nose and eyes by dividing this area two more times.

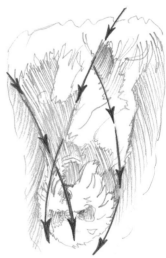

▲ **Step 2** Now that my construction lines are in, I begin to add the dark (positive) shapes. Note how drawing the positive shapes creates the light (negative) shapes. I also take note of the "flow," or movement, in the subject. Follow the arrows I've drawn here, and then look for those flow lines in the final drawing at left. Flow lines not only help you get better proportions (as negative shapes do), they also convey the overall rhythm in a drawing.

Looking for Shapes This sheepdog is a perfect candidate for you to attempt drawing upside down because it is composed of such simple shapes. Lay in the drawing with an HB, and then use a 2B, 4B, and 6B, respectively, for lights, middle values, and darks.

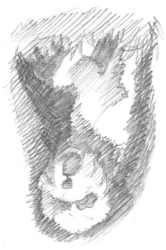

◄ **Step 3** As I slowly refine the edges of both the positive and negative shapes, the sheepdog miraculously begins to appear. But remember, I am drawing abstract shapes, upside down, so I won't know just how accurate my dog really is until I turn it right-side up. Once I am satisfied with the positioning of all the elements, I turn the paper right-side up, and, magically, the dog appears.

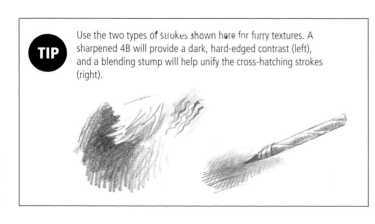

TIP Use the two types of strokes shown here for furry textures. A sharpened 4B will provide a dark, hard-edged contrast (left), and a blending stump will help unify the cross-hatching strokes (right).

DRAWING VALUES AS SHAPES

This demonstration is a summation of all the shape- and value-seeing tools I have discussed so far. You can attempt copying it either right-side up or upside down. If it looks too difficult, I recommend you try drawing it upside down. Stick with the basics and avoid preconceptions, and you will be amazed at what you can accomplish.

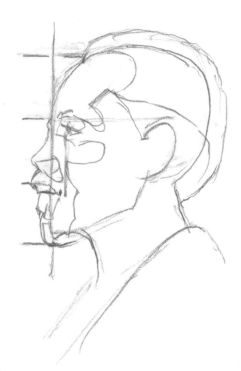

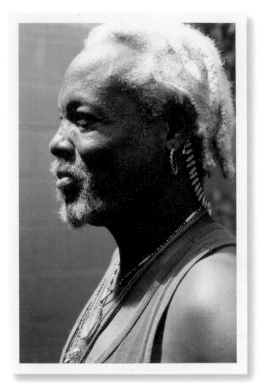

Observing the Subject Before I start drawing, I observe my subject and look for basic shapes and measurements.

Step 1 With an HB pencil, I lightly sketch a vertical line and mark off three equal divisions: hairline to brow, brow to top of lip, and top of lip to bottom of beard. I draw the basic shape of the head and place the nose and lips on the left side of the vertical plumb line; then I sketch in the shapes of the shadows.

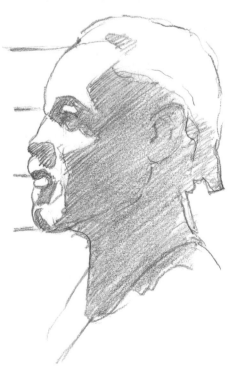

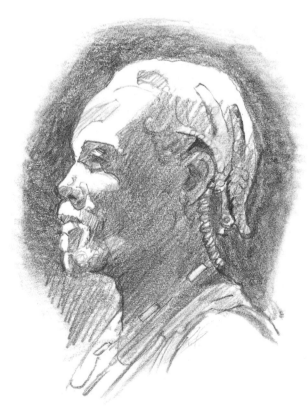

Step 2 I erase the construction lines and carefully shade the shadow shapes with one flat tone. I don't bother with details at this point; instead, I concentrate on shading the light and dark shapes as accurately as possible.

Step 3 This is the stage where I render details and the smallest shapes. Shown in profile, the features are relatively simple and clearly can be seen as light and dark relationships. If I accurately draw these shapes, I can achieve a likeness.

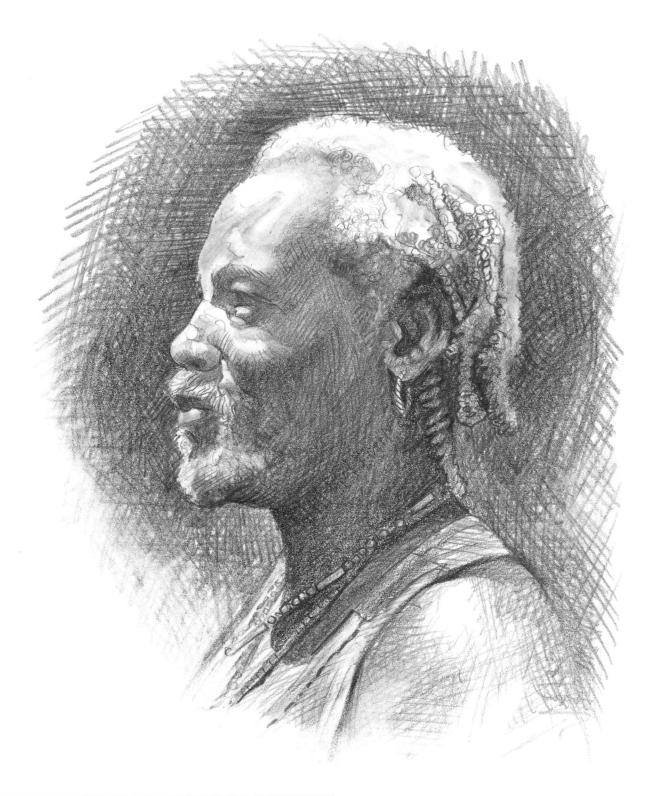

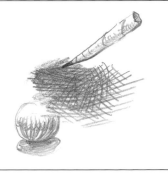

Step 4 I employ various strokes and blends to suggest textures and
transitions in value. I primarily use crosshatching to complete the drawing of
this head. But these are not just random strokes. If you look at the chin and
cheek, you will notice that the stroke directions not only add darkness but also
help define the multiple curves of these areas.

DEPICTING FORM

Light and shadow create the illusion of solidity, or form, in drawing. This exercise will help you observe the light and shadow "families," or groups of values, in any composition.

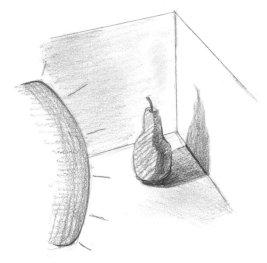

Step 1 Set up your still life box, place a pear or another object in the corner of the box, and shine a spotlight on the side of the object to create a division of light and shadow.

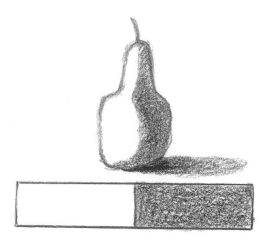

Step 2 Draw the pear with a simple division between light and shadow. The value scale below the pear demonstrates this division.

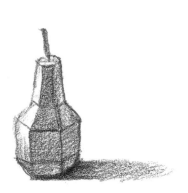

Step 3 Now look for planes. Any planes that are mostly illuminated by the direct light are part of the light family. Planes facing away from the light—including the cast shadow—are part of the shadow family. Make another sketch of the pear, showing each plane, and shade only the planes in the shadow family.

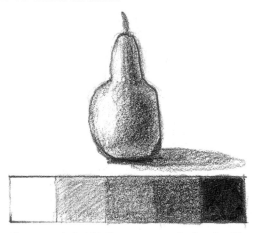

Step 4 Draw the pear again, but this time use a range of values. By adding subtle halftones between the extremes of light and dark, you can create a feeling of solid roundness.

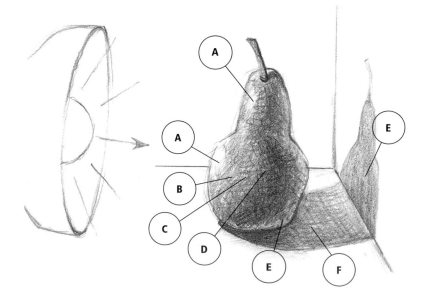

Understanding Terms This illustration shows the terms used to describe the lights and shadows that create form. The very light areas, A, are *highlights* (which are fairly subtle on a pear). B is a *light* area surrounding the highlights. C is a *halftone;* it forms the important visual transition between light and shadow. D is the *shadow core,* or the area where light ceases and shadow begins. E is *reflected light,* both on the wall (within the cast shadow) and on the object (along the core shadow). Without the contrast provided by reflected light on the dark side of the pear, there would be no shadow core—only shadow. F is the *cast shadow,* which begins dark and hard-edged and grows lighter and less distinct as it recedes from the light source and object.

Directing the Eye with Value Edges

Value edges, or the lines where contrasting values meet, play an important role in directing the eye around a drawing and holding the viewer's attention.

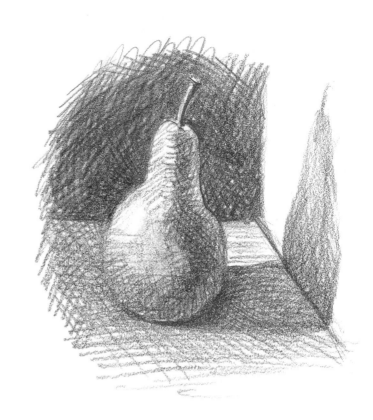

▶ **Establishing a Focal Point** When value contrast is high and hard edges dominate one area, the viewer's eye will be directed to that area. This area is called the "focal point," and it should also be the center of interest.

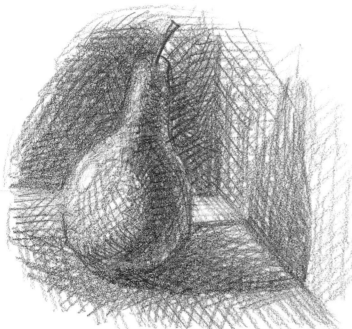

◀ **Capturing Attention** Medium values and medium edges create secondary areas of importance. A picture should primarily contain these elements, so the hard-edged focal point will stand out and seize the viewer's attention.

▶ **Representing the Periphery** Close values and soft edges represent the periphery of vision. When you look directly at an object, everything else is mostly out of focus. If you keep the least important areas of your drawing soft edged, the viewer's eye will then travel to the hard-edged contrasts of the more important areas.

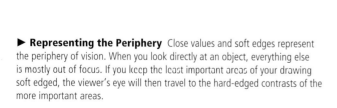

ARRANGING VALUES

Now that you understand the importance of learning to see your subject as a series of dark and light shapes rather than as an identifiable "thing" with a label, let's experiment with setting up a composition using a still life box. (See page 5 for a description of how to construct a still life box.) As an example, I have set up a still life using a light, a medium, and a dark object to show how a setup with balanced values is affected by three very different backgrounds.

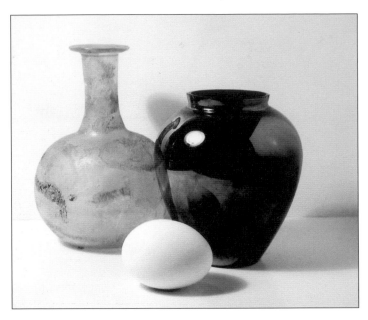

◄ **Light Background** With white making up all of the negative space (the walls and floor), the edges of all three objects are very sharp, except where the white egg meets the white floor. Note how the light becomes slightly darker on the right as it gets farther from its spotlight source. This is characteristic of artificial light.

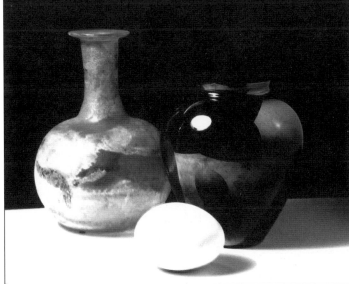

► **Light/Dark Background** Now I add a piece of black mat board to the walls of the box, leaving the floor white. What a difference! The dark edges of the black vase are now lost, and the cast shadows appear darker because there is less ambient light bouncing into them. (A photographic note: By exposing for such a bright white on the base, the subtle core shadow on the egg becomes washed out.)

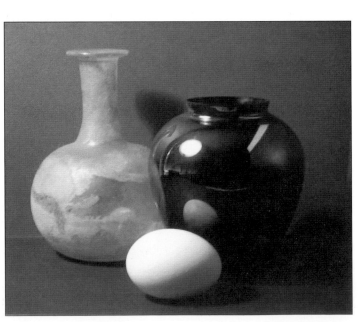

◄ **Uniformly Dark Background** For this setup, I cover the two walls of the box with a nearly middle-value gray and the bottom of the box with a black mat board. The bottom appears to be dark gray rather than black because the bright spotlight lightens it. Notice how the reflection in the black vase is nearly absent now (except for a little light from an overhead fluorescent lamp), and the values of all three objects appear more subtle.

Drawing a Simple Still Life

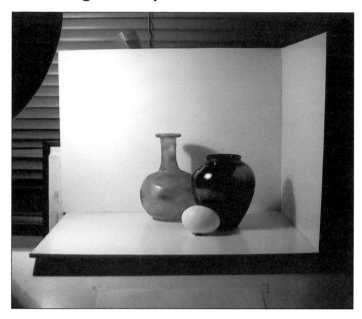

Setting Up a Still Life To start this exercise, either arrange your own still life or copy my setup, and place the objects in the still life box. Position your light source above and to one side of the box. (We will cover more about light sources on the following pages.)

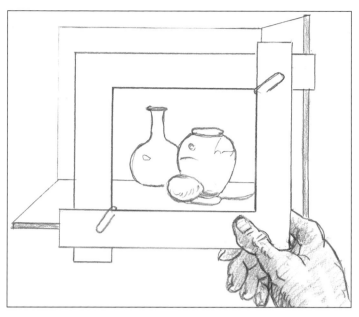

Selecting a Composition After choosing a light background for my drawing, I create a viewfinder (see "Making a Viewfinder" below) to help me determine the best format. When I like what I see, I lightly sketch the composition onto my paper, using the measuring techniques described on page 11.

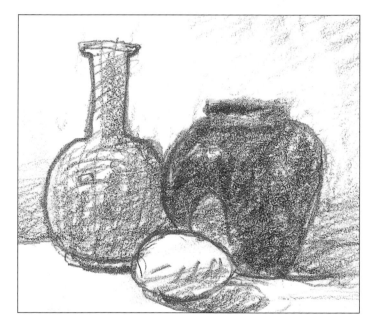

Creating Thumbnails Before continuing with my drawing, I make a few small, quick, rough sketches on scrap paper to test out the values in my composition. These *thumbnail studies* help me decide what values will work best for my final drawing.

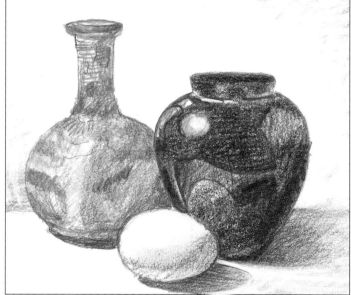

Building Up Correct Values Returning to my paper, I use sidestrokes, crosshatching, a stump, and a kneaded eraser to build up the desired values. To get very light, textured values, I lightly smudge an area and then lift out lights with my kneaded eraser.

Making a Viewfinder

Use two L-shaped pieces of cardboard (paper-clipped together; see illustration above) as you would a viewfinder on a camera to help find the best arrangement for your composition. Look through the frame; move it closer and farther away, or rotate it until you find the most pleasing view.

ESTABLISHING A LIGHT SOURCE

Most indoor situations have too many light sources to make a good drawing from life. Ambient light from windows, lamps, open doors, and so on produces conflicting highlights and makes it difficult to show solidity. A single, controlled light source works best.

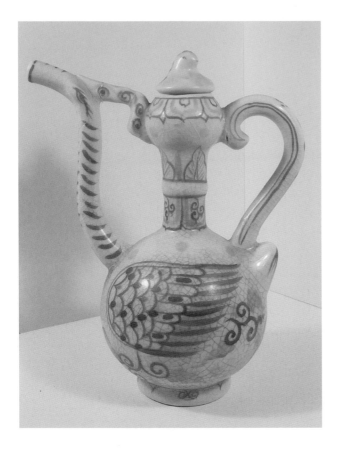

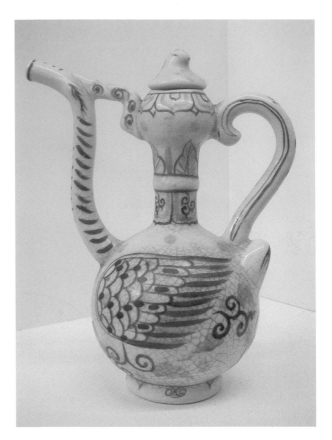

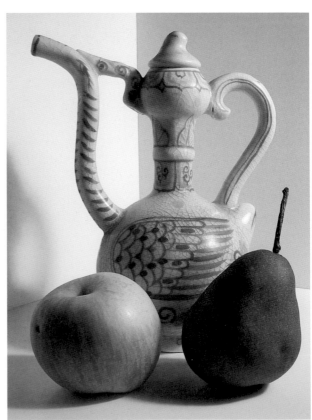

Double Lighting (above) Two opposing incandescent sources light this Asian teapot, creating two highlights and two vague shadows. Compare this photo to the solidity of the form on pages 24 and 25. The double lighting makes the teapot look flat.

Fluorescent Lighting (above right) Because they come from a long-wave light source, fluorescent lights tend to diffuse and soften forms. Here, the teapot is set in the same place as in the first photo, but now all the light is coming from eight-foot fluorescent bulbs above. As with other multiple light sources, the result is that the teapot still appears too flat to make an interesting drawing.

Single Lighting (right) In this version, I add an apple and a pear for variety of shapes, values, and surface types. I light the setup from the right and slightly above. The pot and apple are fairly glossy, so their highlights are bright, but the pear has a matte surface, which diffuses its highlight. Compared to the first two setups, the light, shadows, and cast shadows in this setup not only add a sense of volume but also create an interesting design.

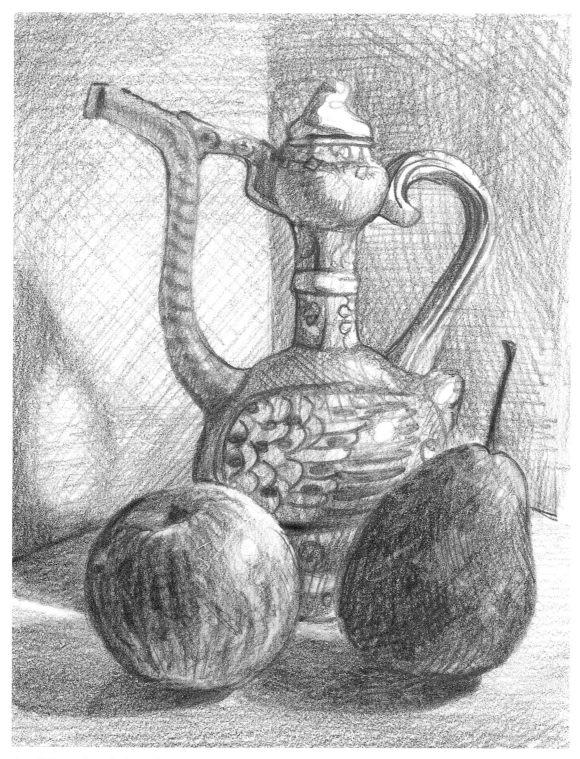

▲ **Building and Gradating Values** I use HB, 2B, and 4B pencils and a single light source for this rendering of the composition at left. I employ crosshatching to build up values, and I use underhand sidestrokes for gradated areas.

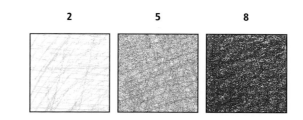

| 2 | 5 | 8 |

▶ **Value Scale** This drawing makes use of values 2, 5, and 8.

REINTERPRETING VALUES

When an amateur photographer points a camera at a bright sky or glaring ocean and clicks, the darks in the resulting image can end up too dark, and the lights are often washed out. The optimum exposure for a camera—and for the human eye—is middle-value gray. An artist must understand this phenomenon when working from a photo and attempt to correct the values accordingly.

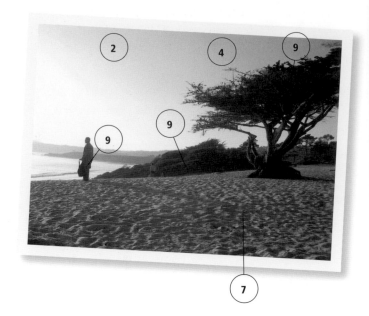

▶ **Adapting from a Photo** Compare this photo with my drawing below, and note how the readjusted values in the drawing add more balance and atmosphere. I employ a full range of values, but the darkest darks serve solely as accents in the tree and the human figure.

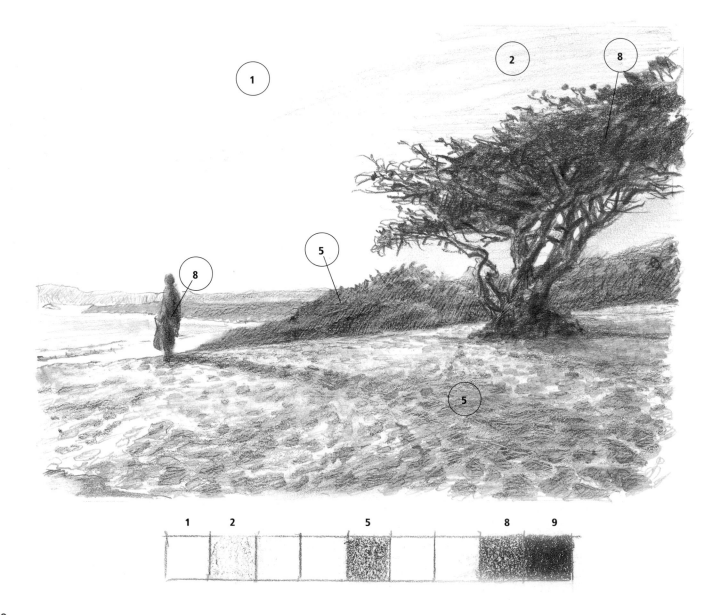

Adjusting Value "Keys"

Like a pianist, an artist can choose any "key" and play in it. A virtuoso musician knows how to use different keys to evoke different emotions. Similarly, by using value variations, artists can convey a range of moods, from bright and cheery to dark and somber, or even portray weather conditions and times of day. Think of a value scale as a piano keyboard, with each group of numbered values representing a different key.

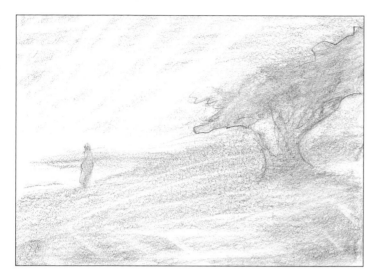

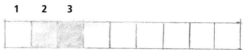

◀ **High Key** When you keep your values on the upper (lighter) side of the scale, the effect will be that of a foggy morning. It could also evoke a dreamy, pensive feeling from the viewer. This drawing makes use of values 1, 2, and 3.

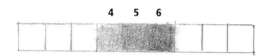

▶ **Middle Key** Limiting yourself to the middle part of the scale creates the look of a cloudy day. These middle values can create a calm, soothing atmosphere. This drawing makes use of values 4, 5, and 6.

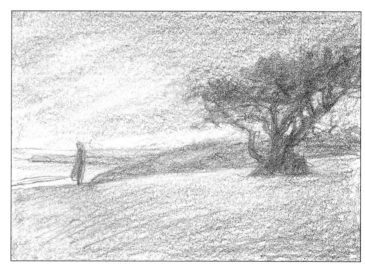

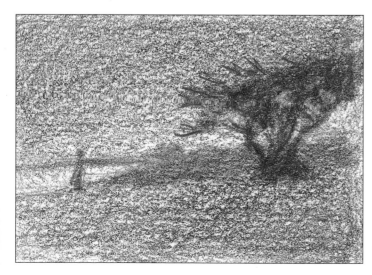

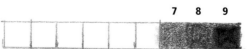

◀ **Low Key** The lower (darker) part of the scale is perfect for depicting dusk, dawn, or a stormy day. Emotions elicited from this drawing could range from peaceful and tranquil to passionate and turbulent, depending on the intensity of the darks. This drawing makes use of values 7, 8, and 9.

USING CONTRAST TO ATTRACT THE EYE

In a successful conversation, we make our point by getting right to it and stating it clearly. Drawing is the same in this respect. By placing your center of interest (or focal point) carefully and giving it the greatest amount of contrast, you can create visual interest and draw in the viewer's eye. The point of highest contrast immediately captures the viewer's attention.

Study these drawings and diagrams to learn how to use contrast and value placement to create both a focal point and a path for the eye to follow.

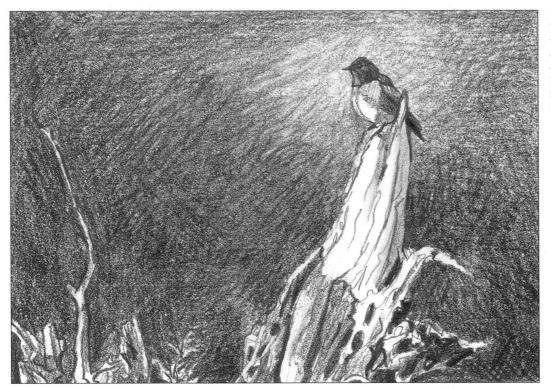

◄ Creating a Focal Point
The viewer's eye immediately goes to the tree trunk and perched bird in this composition because they hold the greatest contrast to the medium-dark background. Notice how I've kept the background a touch lighter behind the bird to better set off the darks.

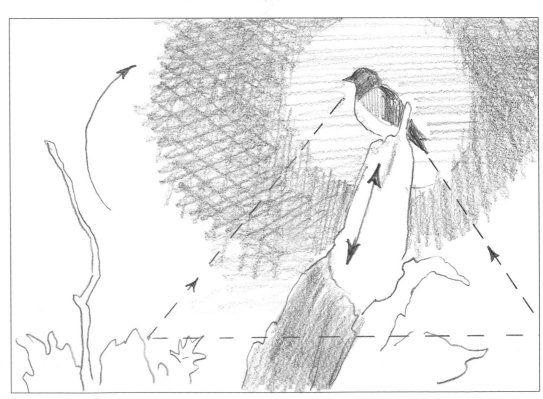

► Circulating the Eye The viewer's eye travels up the thick branch to the high-contrast bird at the apex of a stabilizing triangle. Secondarily, the light branch at far left attracts the eye and holds it, and then circulates the eye back to the bird.

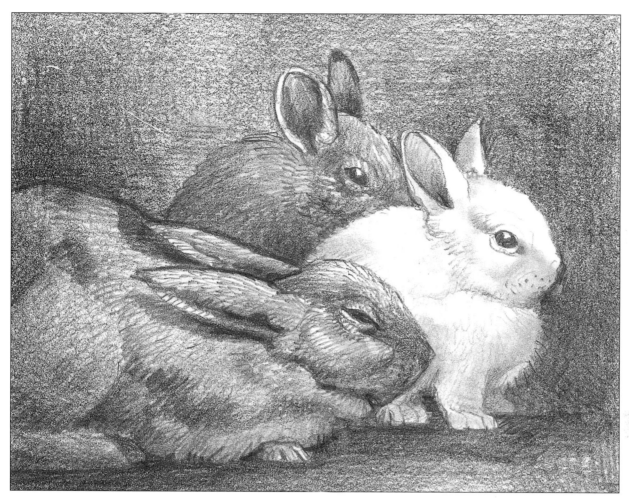

▲ **Centering Interest** By blending the darker rabbits into the background of this drawing, the contrasting white rabbit becomes the center of interest.

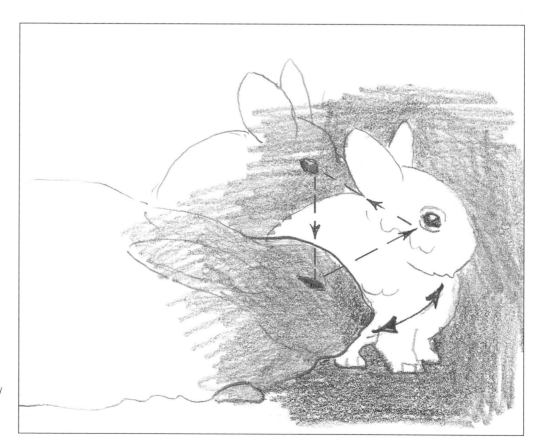

▶ **Directing Attention** The white rabbit's black eye is like a visual magnet; then the beady eyes of the darker rabbits attract the viewer's attention and create a triangular flow between the three rabbits.

MOVING THE EYE THROUGH THE ART

The eye will normally enter a drawing where the largest positive shape touches the border. If such a shape does not touch the border, the eye will jump inside the composition to the most interesting positive element. From this point on, it is the artist's sense of design that will direct the viewer's eye. The eye follows paths created by (1) edges of light and dark; (2) the bulk of light or dark areas; and (3) light or dark dots, dashes, and accents. (For more information, see Chapter 2.)

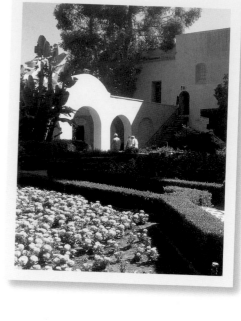

▶ **Attracting and Directing Attention** In this photograph of California mission-style buildings and their surrounding gardens, light guides the viewer's eye into and through the scene. Lines, dots, and accents add interest.

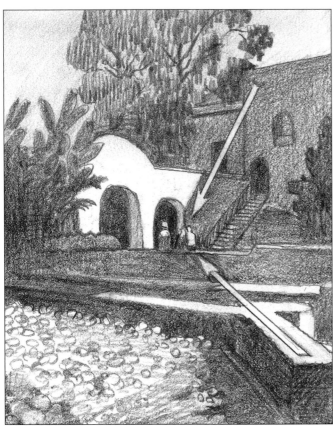

◀ **Drawing Attention** Look at the photo above, and then follow the arrows in this diagram. Note that the eye enters where the foreground hedge touches a border and then moves through the shadow to the people, who act as accents. Speaking of interest, cover up the flowers with your hand, and see how much sparkle the picture would lose if they were eliminated.

▶ **Maintaining Interest** Have you ever looked at a long, blank wall or an empty sky? Think of how your eye begs for something solid to focus on. It cannot stay in one place for very long. Like a playful kitten fascinated by a rolling ball of yarn, the eye is attracted to accents of light and edges. Without these, the eye will simply become bored and move on to someone else's drawing. Once again look at the photo; analyze how your eye moves within it, and see if the arrows in this diagram are similar to the paths your eye follows.

CREATING DEPTH

Linear perspective lends the illusion of dimension to a composition, but an artist has additional tools: overlapping objects, creating contrasts in value and texture, using aerial perspective, and introducing shadows.

Using Shapes, Values, and Textures

The way you place values in the foreground, middle ground, and background affects the perception of depth in a drawing. Contrasting these values and their textures conveys a sense of dimension.

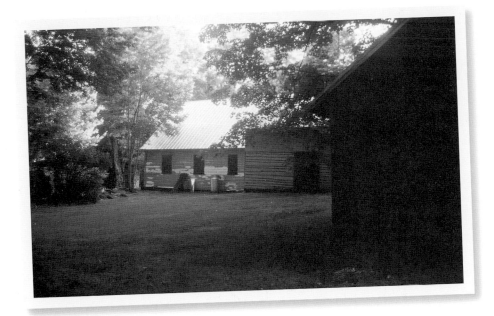

▲ **Adjusting References** In my photo above, the foreground came out too dark because the camera's exposure was adjusted for the bright sky in the background. To create a more balanced composition, I use this photo to create two thumbnail sketches (below), each with a different value arrangement from which to choose.

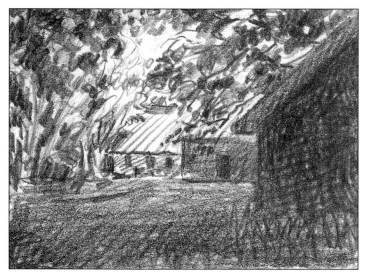

◄ **Overlapping Shapes** Overlapping is an excellent way to create the appearance of depth. The addition of aerial perspective (see page 38) increases the illusion further. Although the composition shows depth, it still lacks interest because it remains overly true to the photograph. The composition also is unbalanced with the dark right side drawing the viewer's eye.

► **Balancing Value Contrasts** Starting again, I use the same value structure as I did for the first thumbnail. However, I lighten the foreground shed, add a door and a window, draw some branches in front to push back the shed, and add lighter grass in front of the distant building to create a balance of value contrasts throughout. I find this thumbnail more interesting, so I will use it in conjunction with the photo as the basis of my final rendering.

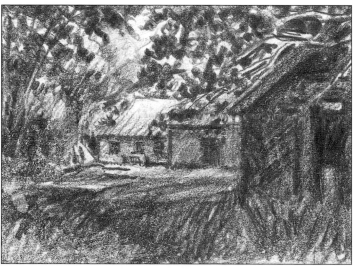

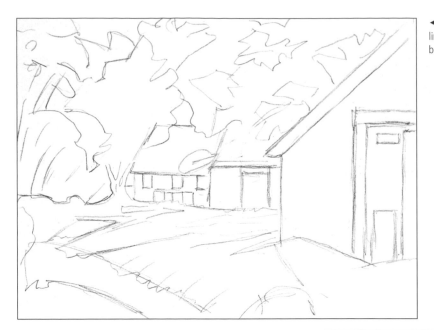

◀ **Step 1** Sketching lightly with an HB pencil and using primarily straight lines, I mark out the foreground shed with the new details, two distant buildings, diagonals on the ground, and general areas of foliage.

▶ **Step 2** Now I transform the light, straight lines into more specific shapes and details. Using a softer 2B pencil, I darken the contour lines and apply a flat tone over the entire composition, except for the light areas in the sky and the roof of the background building.

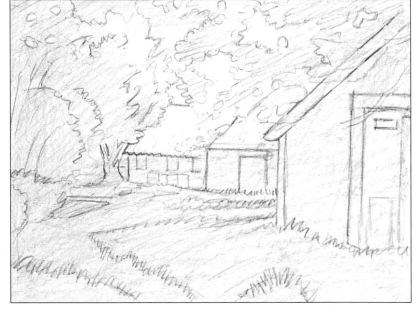

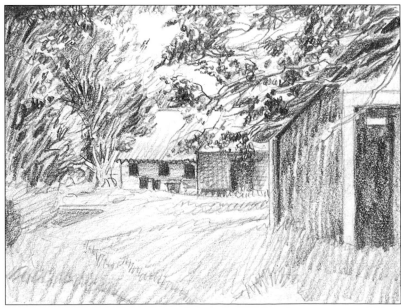

◀ **Step 3** In order to set the range of my value scale, I use a 4B pencil to darken the windows, the shed door, and some of the branches and leaves. This tells me where to place my middle values, as the lights and darks already are established.

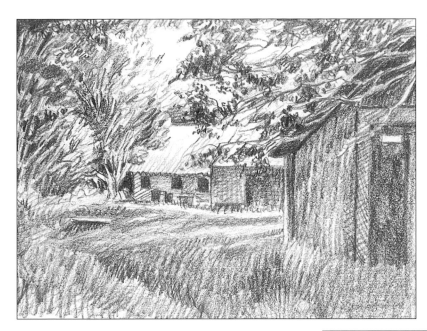

◄ **Step 4** I continue to darken the meadow and its diagonal lines with crosshatching. Using an underhand shading stroke in the trees, I darken the largest areas with blending strokes. This brings out the light, which I can further accentuate with a kneaded eraser.

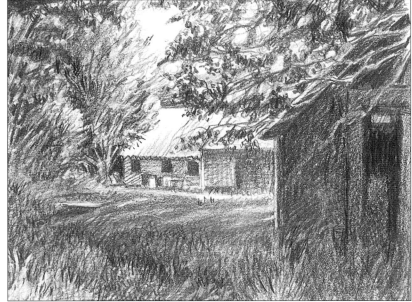

► **Step 5** To complete the rendering, I bring out the lighter and darker values to emphasize the focal point and imbue it with an intimate, inviting atmosphere. Note how the detailed textures and dark values in the foreground push the lighter distant structures into the background. This is an example of aerial perspective (see page 38).

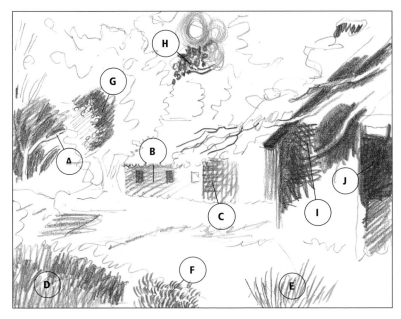

◄ **Contrasting Textures** This is a sampling of the various strokes I use to build textural interest in this drawing: On the left and right sides, I darken around light areas and then blend over parts to make branches (A). Light cross-hatching on the distant building (B) and heavier crosshatching on the middle structure (C) enhance the perspective in the rendering. I employ medium lines (D), long lines (E), and grassy texture (F) to lend interest to the foreground vegetation. Dark, blended strokes (G) and dots (H) work well for the trees in the background. For the near shed, I use dark crosshatching (I) and heavy dark strokes (J). (See "Basic Strokes" on page 14 for additional textures.)

Employing Aerial Perspective and Shadows

In nature, impurities in the air (such as moisture and dust) block out some rays of sunlight, making objects in the distance appear less distinct than objects in the foreground. This phenomenon is referred to as "aerial perspective," and it creates the illusion of depth. In this quiet scene, I take advantage of both aerial perspective and foreground shadows give my drawing dimension.

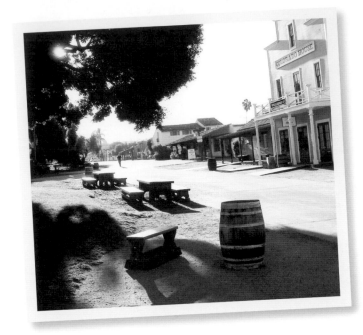

◄ **Choosing a Scene** This location is more interesting in the summer when long shadows come from the side, but the only photo I have was shot in winter with the sun coming in from the south. My solution? I simply shift the direction of the shadows by modifying the composition to match my summer memory. Despite the limitations of the photo, I still can use it to reference when building an appealing composition.

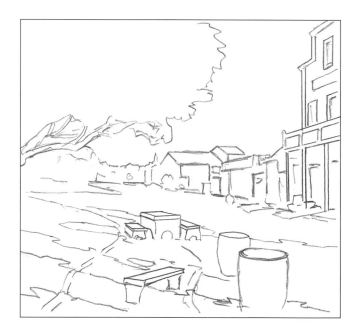

► **Thumbnail Sketch** Before starting the actual rendering, I draw a thumbnail sketch. After I block in the basic shapes, I lay in the new, summer shadow areas. My intention is to lead the viewer's eye into the scene by establishing dark, contrasting shadows across the foreground. This thumbnail is now my value guide; the photo is only a reference for the shapes and details.

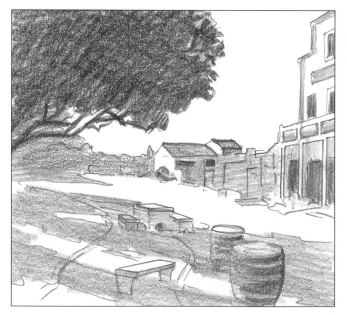

◄ **Rough Value Study** Now I shade in the three main values I intend to use: The tree is the darkest value, the shadows and background are middle values, and the rest is light. This is not a final, detailed value study—just a rough guide for me to recognize the light and dark families as I proceed toward the final rendering shown on page 41.

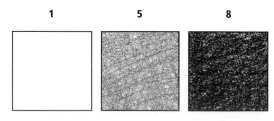

1	5	8

▲ **Value Scale** I use values 1, 5, and 8 in this drawing.

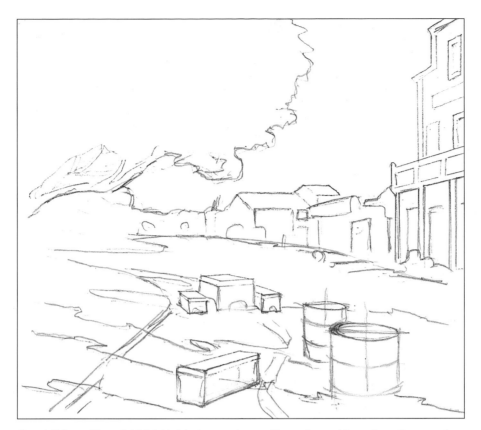

Step 1 Using an HB pencil, I lightly block in the general composition, paying special attention to the perspective on the benches, table, and barrels. These shapes, if drawn correctly, will give an indication of the artist's eye level, which is slightly above them.

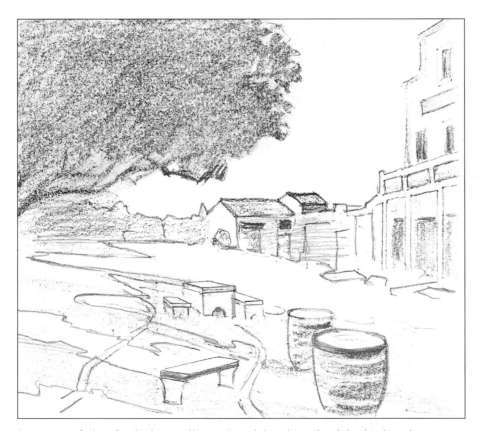

Step 2 Now I further refine the shapes and begin to lay in darker values with underhand strokes. I do not get as dark as the value study yet because I still need to be sure that the shapes of the foreground shadows are placed correctly.

39

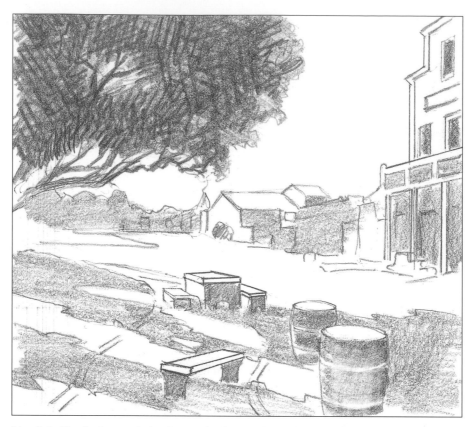

Step 3 At this point, I am certain that these are the shapes I will retain for the final drawing, so I take out my softer 2B and 4B pencils and carefully refine the areas of value. Now the darkest shadows are about as dark as the value study, and now I can focus on adding textures while maintaining the correct values.

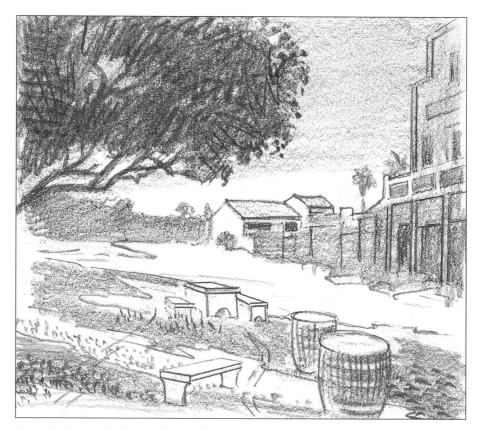

Step 4 At this stage, I begin to experiment with various textures, but I do not completely finish any particular area. I add details such as palm trees in the background, the gradated sky, and the dark windows and doorways.

► **Adding Textures** Here are the strokes I use to finish the drawing: I darken the tree with 4B and 6B pencils, combining sidestrokes and cross-hatching (A). For the sky, I combine sidestrokes, linear strokes, and some erasing to lift out lighter streaks (B). For the background, I use sidestrokes and an eraser (C). For the grassy area in the foreground, I use sidestrokes and grassy strokes (D). I darken the barrel with sidestrokes and linear, vertical strokes (E). The dirt is—appropriately—dirt texture (F). (See "Basic Strokes" on page 14 for additional textures and strokes.)

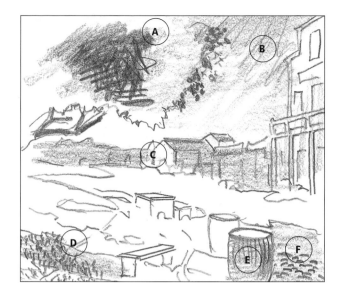

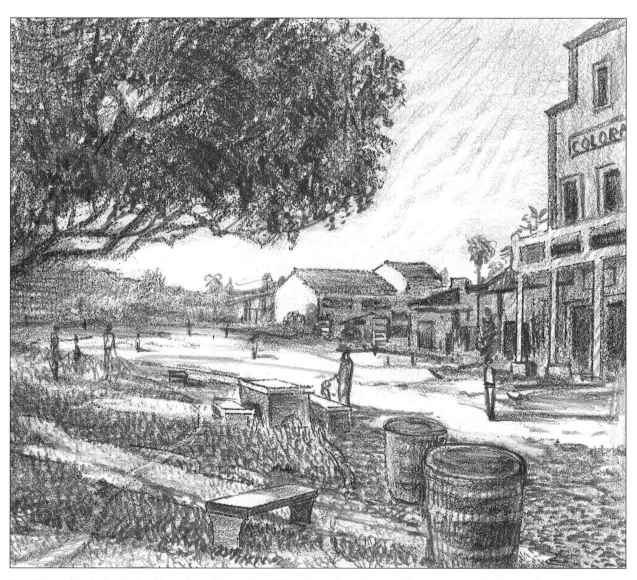

Step 5 I complete the drawing by adding value and texture. The addition of larger figures in the middle ground and smaller figures in the background helps create depth. Note how I've employed aerial perspective by giving the objects in the foreground the most detail. The darker foreground shadows add to the illusion of depth by contrasting the lighter middle ground and background.

CAPTURING LIGHT ON BLACK-AND-WHITE

On page 16 we discussed the phenomenon of simultaneous contrast—where a middle value looks darker on white than it does on black. We also explored the strength of black-and-white images in conveying shape, as well as the way that adding an extra value or two transforms a flat shape into a three-dimensional form. But how does an artist show volume on black? This photograph of a zebra's head offers a perfect opportunity to show the thought process involved in solving this problem.

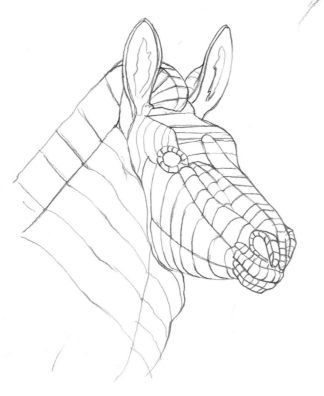

◄ Working with Strong Contrasts
This subject presents a challenge in depicting the contrast between black and white without flattening the shape of the zebra's head.

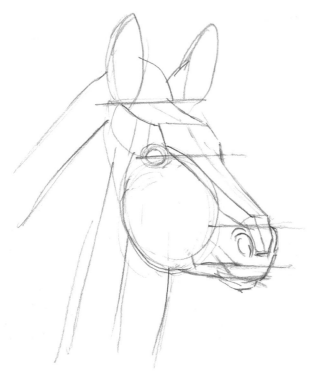

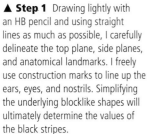

▲ Step 1 Drawing lightly with an HB pencil and using straight lines as much as possible, I carefully delineate the top plane, side planes, and anatomical landmarks. I freely use construction marks to line up the ears, eyes, and nostrils. Simplifying the underlying blocklike shapes will ultimately determine the values of the black stripes.

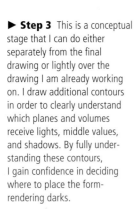

► Step 3 This is a conceptual stage that I can do either separately from the final drawing or lightly over the drawing I am already working on. I draw additional contours in order to clearly understand which planes and volumes receive lights, middle values, and shadows. By fully understanding these contours, I gain confidence in deciding where to place the form-rendering darks.

▲ Step 2 Before continuing, I check the proportions from step 1. Once they are correct, I carefully go over the straight lines and transform them into light, accurate, outer contours. I soften and delineate the blocks and cylinders on the head so I know exactly where they should go. This will be my "road map" for shading the forms.

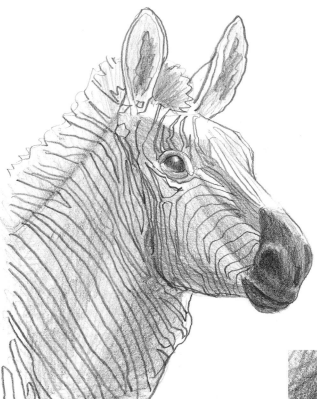

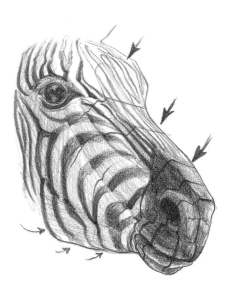

► **Capturing Variations in Value** Study the lines, contours, and arrows in this drawing. A bright source of light bleaches out the dark stripes that face upward toward the light; those same stripes darken in value as they curve away from the light. Also note how reflected light bounces back up to the underside of the head. By capturing these variations in value, you convey the underlying form of your subject.

 Step 4 I outline the stripes before shading them. Now I am ready to subtly shade the planes and cylinders that were established in steps 2 and 3.

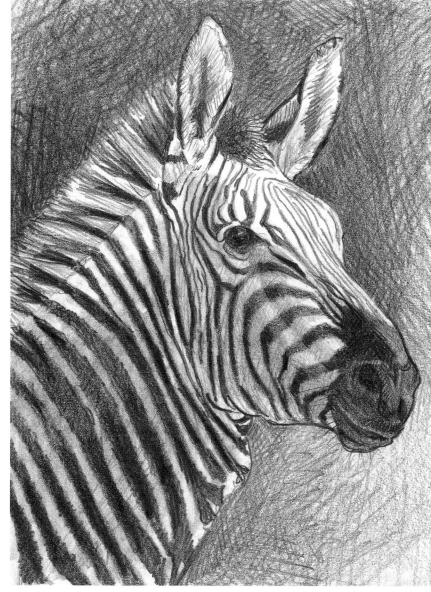

TIP

If you find the stripes too complicated to freehand, make a copy of the photo the same size as your drawing paper, and then transfer the stripes from the photo onto tracing paper. Place the tracing paper against a bright window, tape your drawing over it, and trace the stripes.

► **Step 5** Compare this drawing to step 3 and the detail (above right). The important correlation between the drawing at right and the other two is the way the changing value on the black stripes in this drawing reveals the structure that was rendered with contour lines in the others. Artists call this principle "local value": As light and shadow hit the forms and the black stripes overlaying them, the black stripes appear lighter or darker. This consistency in change of value reveals form, rather than flattening it.

COMBINING THE ELEMENTS OF DESIGN

Line, value, texture, shape, size, and direction are the elements or main ingredients of which every drawing is made. As an artist, you must decide how and why each element should be used. On the following pages, I separately analyze and describe each element of this seascape. As you study each individual diagram, compare it with the final rendering on this page to see how each element functions properly in context with the others.

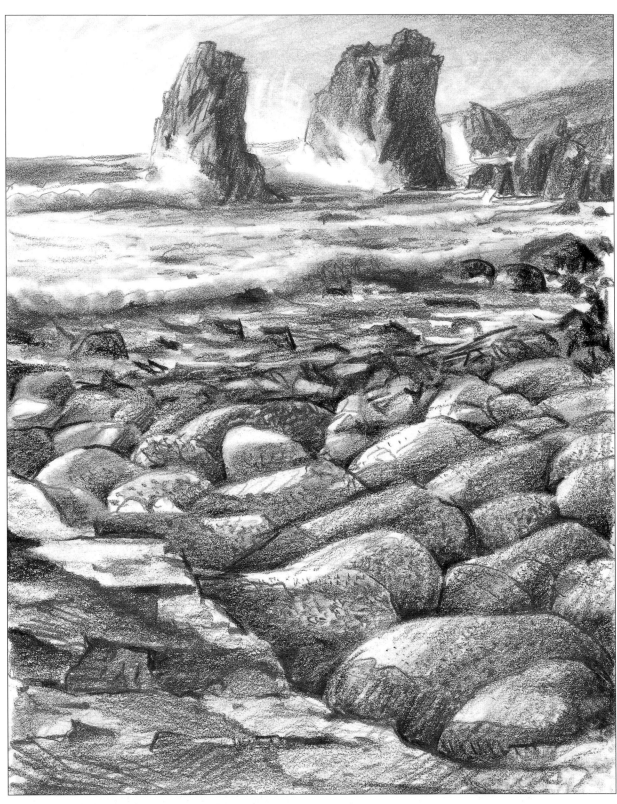

Making Use of Design Elements This seascape makes effective use of each of the elements of design. Over the next three pages, you'll see how each of the elements is used.

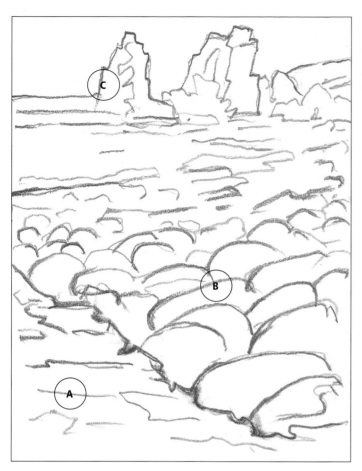

◄ Line You learned on page 17 that lines do not exist in nature; they only exist in the two-dimensional world of drawing. Lines in this seascape are mainly used to separate values of light and dark. In the foreground, a variety of thick and thin lines adds textural complexity and interest (A). The lines around the boulders separate the foreground and background planes (B). The distant rocks use lines to show crevices on the sunlit side (C).

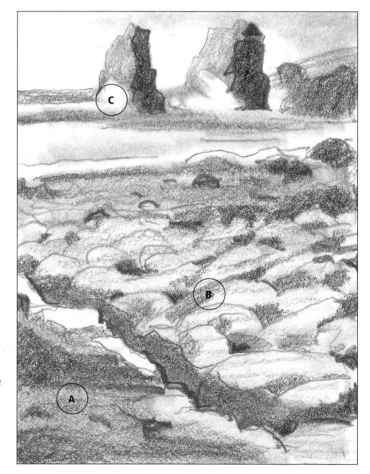

► Value Never underestimate the importance of value in drawing. I would even venture to say that it is the most important of all the elements. Shapes, lines, and textures hold little interest without variations in value. The distant rocks are the center of interest, so they stand in greatest contrast to the lightest lights (C). The middle-ground boulders are basically middle values with only small accents of light and dark (B). The foreground rocks possess the same value as the more distant boulders, but they are shaped differently to avoid monotony (A).

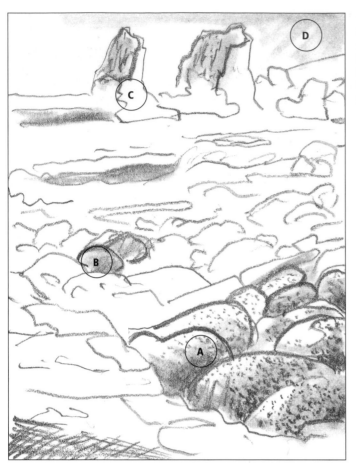

◄ **Texture** Conveying texture is a challenge because it is an invention of descriptive strokes. Texture is an antidote for monotony but can itself become monotonous if overemphasized. The foreground boulders are granite; small dots show their texture effectively (A). Farther back, the rocks become more atmospheric, and their textures become softer, with fewer dots (B). The distant rocks are a blend of dark softness and small linear markings because they need to stay atmospheric (C). The sky is shaded softly with lights lifted out with an eraser (D).

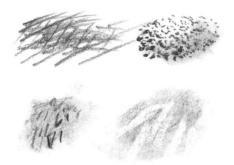

▲ **Seascape Textures** The textures I used for this seascape are shown above. (Also see "Basic Strokes" on page 14 for additional textures and strokes.)

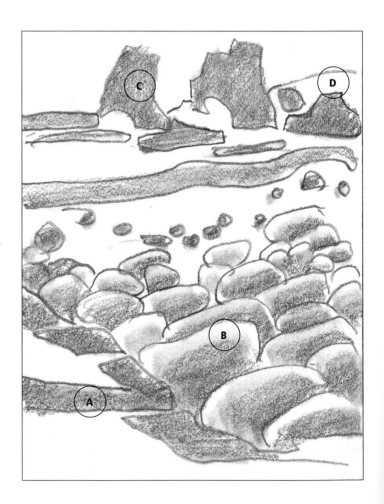

► **Shape** I find it useful to identify shapes as square, round, and triangular, or Modifications and combinations of these three basic categories. (See "Understanding Value and Shape" on page 15 for examples of these and other shapes.) None of the shapes in this seascape are clear-cut. The shapes in the foreground are short or long rectangular variations of a square (A). The boulders are round and oval variations of a rectangle (B). The distant rocks in the center are variants of a square (C), and the distant rocks on the right come closer to being triangular (D). Variations in size and value are key in eliminating monotony.

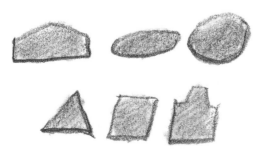

▲ **Seascape Shapes** The simple shapes that make up this seascape are shown above.

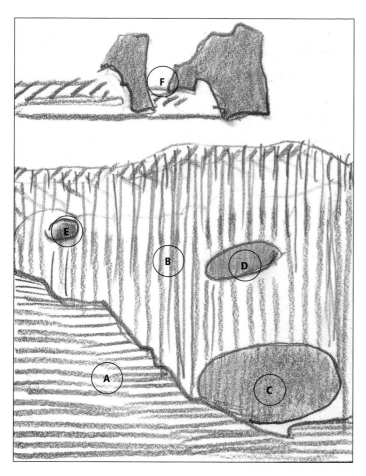

◄ Size In this seascape, size refers to both positive and negative shapes, especially in relation to the contrast between large and small. The eye requires variation to remain engaged, and a successful drawing keeps the viewer engaged. The smaller foreground area (A), with its diagonal, hard, straight edge, sets off the larger, softer area with its rounded boulders (B). The foreground boulders (C), middle-ground boulders (D), and background boulders (E) become progressively smaller, suggesting depth. The distant rocks differ slightly in size against the rectangular negative space (F).

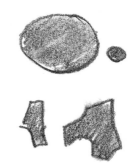

▲ Varying Sizes Variations in size provide interest in your artwork.

► Direction Vertical, diagonal, and horizontal lines all engender emotional responses. A vertical direction expresses austerity and uprightness. Diagonal thrusts imply movement and dynamism. A horizontal line conveys tranquility and repose. All three directions are present in this seascape. Diagonal thrusts provide movement into the picture (B). The diagonal thrust is gently tempered by a counter-diagonal (C) and a horizontal foreground movement (A) that echoes the stable horizon (E). As diagonal thrusts come closer to the horizon, they flatten out and become more passive, as laws of perspective dictate they should (D). Finally, verticals reflect the overall uprightness of the picture itself (F).

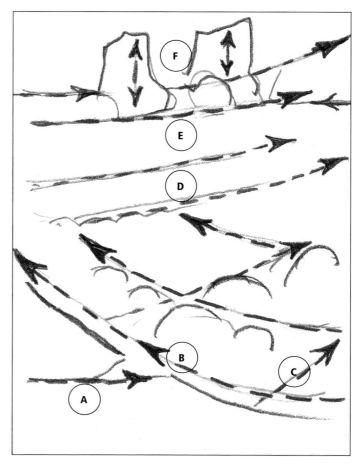

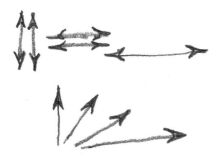

▲ Primary Directions The three main directions of movement are diagonal, horizontal, and vertical.

PULLING IT ALL TOGETHER

This straightforward portrait sums up many of the lessons you've learned. The reminders on the next page are important to remember because they cover the essence of building up any drawing.

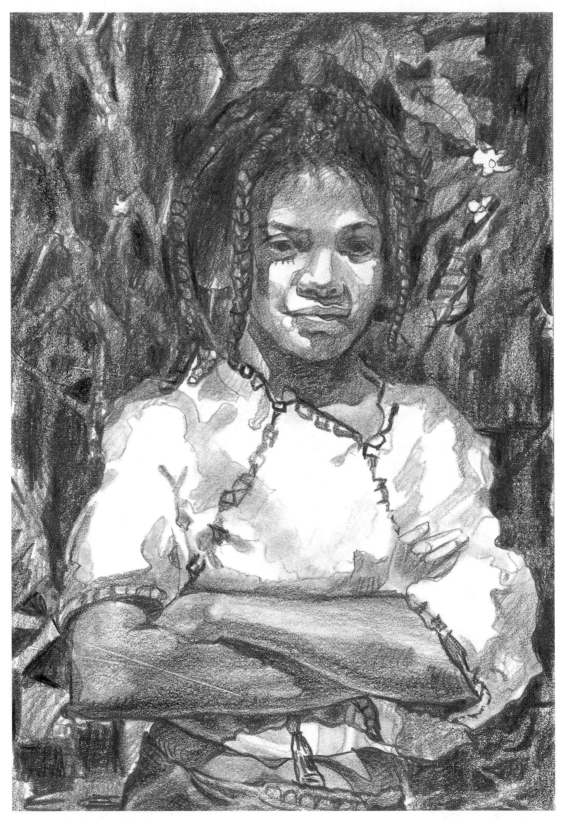

The Sum of Many Parts To create this portrait, I first establish the basic values and shapes of the composition. Then I add texture and refine the lines, shapes, and values.

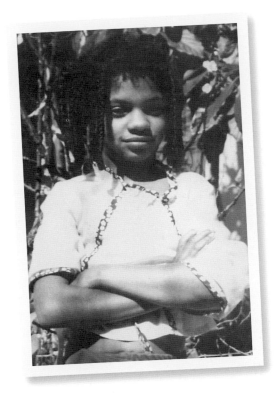

Modifying the Original Image This is a good photo from which to work, but the background is a bit distracting. The solution is to eliminate conflicting whites, then darken and unify the background.

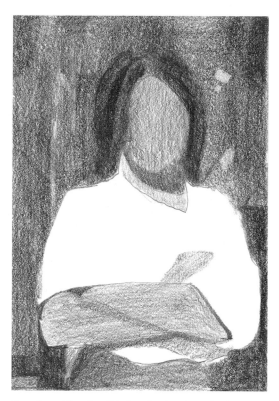

Creating a Thumbnail Value Study When I decide to reinterpret a photo, small thumbnail drawings direct me to my next interpretation. I still use the photo for details, but the value study becomes my reference map for light and dark values.

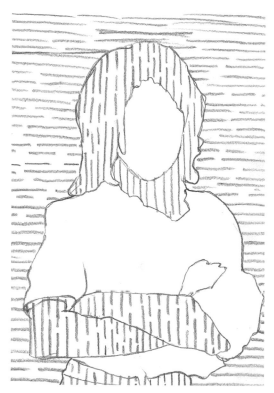

Recognizing Positive and Negative Shapes I block out the large shapes before adding details. Most people think concentration means focusing on a specific detail. To artists, it means focusing on the whole first and the parts later.

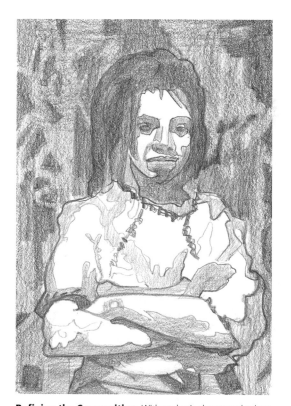

Refining the Composition With my basic shapes and values worked out, I can now fill in the gradations of line, shape, and value that will give the final rendering depth and dimension.

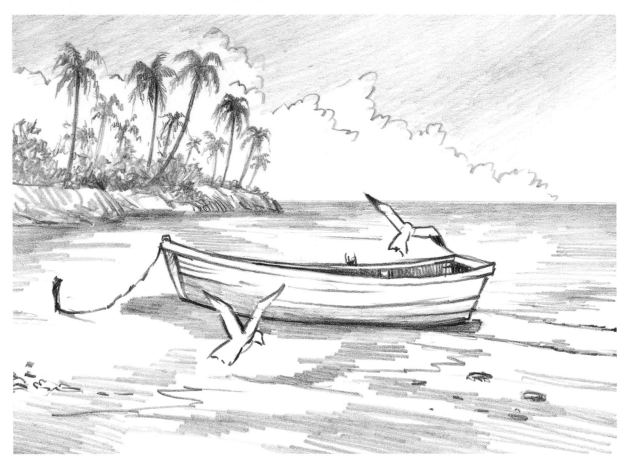

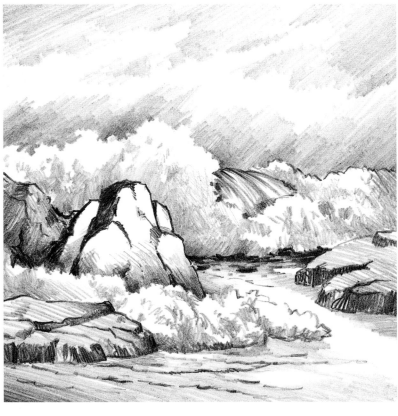

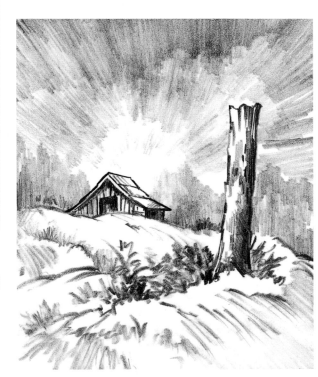

CHAPTER 2

DYNAMIC COMPOSITION

with William F. Powell

The study of composition is important for every aspiring artist. Although some artists say, "Just let it happen, and it will," creating dynamic compositions involves the careful selection of subject matter and placement of elements within the area on which we have chosen to draw (called the "picture plane"). When we decide to make a drawing, we have to ask ourselves some questions: What should this picture say? What is its purpose? What should be included to make my message clear to the viewer? Often we look at a drawing and feel that something about it is not quite right. Although the drawing might look fine for the most part and make proper use of many artistic principles, viewing it is uncomfortable. It does not hold our attention, so we move to the next work of art, looking for a more pleasurable experience and a more interesting composition.

Every picture begins with a simple idea. The final drawing may illustrate that simple idea, or it might grow into an energetic and powerful work—a dynamic composition. To achieve that dynamic quality, you must plan your drawings carefully and apply good compositional principles throughout the process, satisfying the viewer's sense of interest, order, and beauty, while providing a rewarding experience for you.

—William F. Powell

About William F. Powell

William F. Powell is an internationally recognized artist and one of America's foremost colorists. A native of Huntington, West Virginia, Bill has been professionally involved in fine art, commercial art, and technical illustrations for more than 45 years. His experience as an art instructor includes oil, watercolor, acrylic, colored pencil, and pastel—with subjects ranging from landscapes to portraits and wildlife. He also produces instructional art videos.

CHOOSING A VIEWPOINT

After we have selected a subject for our composition, begin by considering viewpoint—the position from which we observe and portray our subject. The viewpoint incorporates the angle of view (from which direction—right, left, or centered—we observe the subject) and the elevation of view (how high or low our position is when viewing the subject). Once these basics have been determined and our composition is finalized, our viewpoint cannot change throughout the drawing process. We must view the subject and all other related elements from the same position at which we started. Objects and structures change greatly, as does the entire composition, if we move from one angle of view or elevation to another.

Angle of View

The viewpoint extends from our eye to the horizon and includes everything we see from a selected, set position. If we move right or left, changing our angle of view, dramatic changes take place in the way we perceive and record the objects and the overall scene. When you are setting up a composition for a drawing, survey your subject from all angles to find the view that will enhance it best. Consider the surrounding elements that you believe will most dynamically highlight the subject. Once these decisions are made, begin refining your composition.

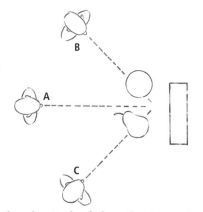

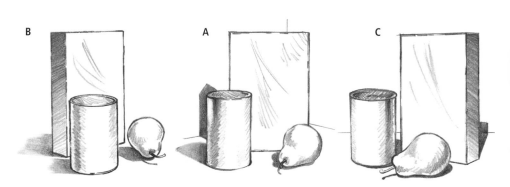

Changing Angle of View Above is an overhead view of an artist looking at a still life composition—a can , a box and a pear—from directly in front of it (A). The dotted lines represent the line of sight. As the artist moves to his left (B) and right (C) to achieve different angles of view, the appearance of the composition changes, as seen in the three illustrations at right.

How the Angle of View Affects the Composition From the A position in the diagram above, the artist sees the composition as it appears in the thumbnail sketch A, shown here. When the artist moves from that angle of view to points B or C, the composition changes as seen here in the left and right sketches; notice the differences in how all the objects appear and relate to one another in these three sketches. Also observe the change in the composition as a whole. Shifting your angle of view changes virtually everything in the composition; thumbnail sketches like these can help you see the differences in your own compositions.

Elevation of View

The elevation of view can be high, level (straight on), or low. From a high angle of view, we look down on the object and see the top and front; in this case, the object's placement on the picture plane is above the horizontal center. In a straight-on view, we see only the front of the object; its position is at eye level, near the middle of the picture plane. But from a low angle of view, we see the bottom and front of the object; its location on the picture plane is below the center.

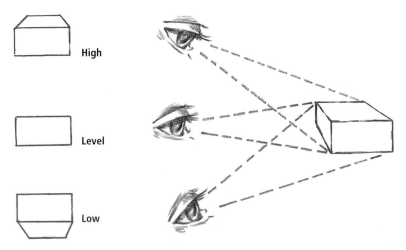

Changing Elevation of View High, level, and low elevation views of the same simple box result in three very different depictions of the subject (shown at the left side of the diagram).

Selecting the Right Elevation

Choosing the correct elevation of view for the subject greatly affects the composition of our drawing. When we view an object from above or below, it looks much different than it does from a level view. The choice of elevation can emphasize the structure of the subject and make a definite statement. For example, a low elevation view of an ocean sunset will emphasize the sky and the sun's rays across it; a high elevation view will highlight the water and the reflections of the sunset; and a level view will result in more equal sky and water elements. Experiment with sketching different subjects from various viewpoints. For each composition, decide which elevation portrays your subject in the most harmonious way. (See examples on this and the following page.)

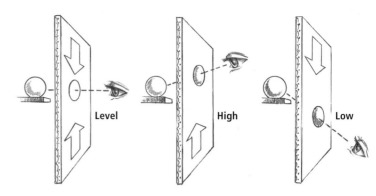

Elevation of View on the Picture Plane These illustrations show how variations in our elevation of view change the subject's position on the picture plane.

Comparing Elevations

Here, we see the same scene from three elevations: high, level, and low. Elevation can dramatically change any subject: landscape, seascape, still life, or portrait.

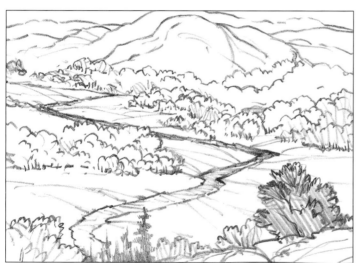

◄ **High Elevation** From a high view, we look down on the entire scene and see many different elements. We see almost no sky; an even higher elevation will totally eliminate the sky, making the landmass appear flatter and giving the river less perspective depth.

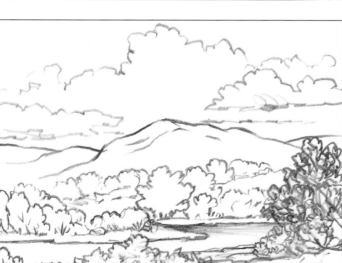

▲ **Level Elevation** In this straight-on (level) view, the length of the river is shortened and flattened. The trees are in a very natural position—the view is just a bit higher than our normal, eye-level view—and we see more sky. The bends of the river become more angular as they recede into the composition. Objects begin to show more size variation due to their placement on the picture plane and relationships with other elements. Distant objects become smaller, as does the width of the river. The top of the mountain almost touches the top of the picture plane.

▲ **Low Elevation** This elevation is slightly lower than eye level, but it is very comfortable to view. There is more of a natural balance here than in the high or level elevations. Make certain that the highest point of the subject is either above or slightly below the true center of the picture plane to avoid monotonous symmetry. The mountaintop here, for instance, appears slightly above the center, considerably lower than in the other views, and we see a great deal of the sky. The low view flattens the river, and the overlapping trees create the illusion of depth in the composition.

Extreme Elevations

For a dramatic effect, try viewing everyday objects from an extremely high viewpoint—a "bird's-eye" view—or a very low elevation—a "worm's-eye" view. Even common subjects look very important from these exaggerated elevations. Try sketching from extreme elevations using small objects, and see how each changes in shape and presentation.

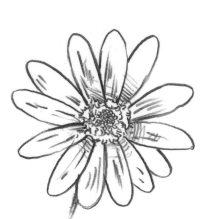

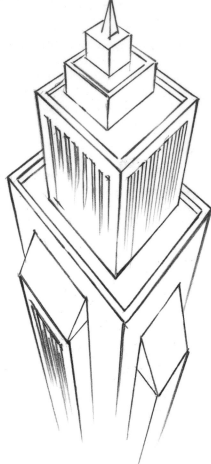

▶ **Seeing from a Bird's-Eye View** This view is even higher than a high-elevation viewpoint, showing the drama of looking down on an object. When looking down on a skyscraper, tremendous change occurs in the building's width; it becomes smaller as it recedes toward the lower floors. The largest portion is the part that is closest to us. If we were directly over the building, we would see none of the sides, only the top portions of each level; for that reason, a slightly angled view best depicts the dramatic qualities. The drawing of the daisy shows a bird's-eye view of a smaller subject. Here we are closer to viewing it straight down and consequently see only a small piece of the stem beneath the flower.

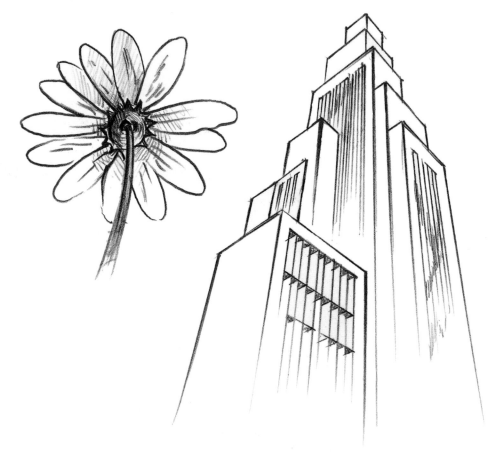

◀ **Seeing From a Worm's-Eye View** Here we have an opposite view of the building and the daisy. We are looking up, as if we were lying on the ground beneath the daisy or standing very close to the building. The worm's-eye view projects a feeling of towering strength to the subject. Notice that the top of the building and the stem on the daisy become smaller as they recede from our viewing point. The worm's-eye view can be just as dramatic in composition planning as the bird's-eye view.

CHOOSING A FORMAT

The two most common formats are vertical (also called "portrait") and horizontal (known as "landscape"), but artists use everything from squares, ovals, and circles to free-form shapes to showcase their drawings. Although some formats are best suited for certain subjects—and vice versa—nearly any format can be used for any subject as long as the drawing is composed correctly. Make simple, small sketches (called "thumbnails") of your subject using different formats; then select the one that makes the best presentation.

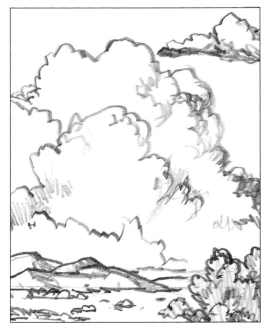

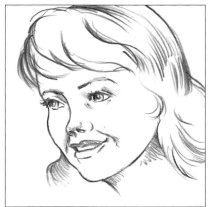

◀ **Square Format** A portrait of a person can be presented in many formats but the vertical or square formats, are best. They allow us to focus the attention on the details of the face.

▲ **Portrait Format** Although this vertical format is called "portrait," it also is a wonderful shape for presenting cloud scenes and skyscapes—notice the low angle of view with large sky areas and just enough foreground to support the sky.

◀ **Landscape Format** A horizontal format provides the width needed for the sweeping panorama of a seascape or landscape. However, it can be just as appropriate for a drawing of your favorite car, flowers, or any subject if the elements are thoughtfully placed.

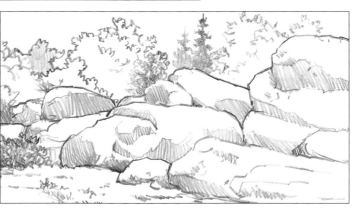

Circular and Oval Formats

Diversify your formats by using circular and oval-shaped formats to showcase subjects in a non-traditional manner. The most important consideration in successfully using these precisely curved picture planes is a good, balanced composition. With the right composition, these formats can accommodate almost any subject. Use a drawing template, computer image, or hand-drawn circle or oval as a picture plane, testing different shapes before selecting one for your composition. Ovals can be used either vertically or horizontally. Although round compositions are very pleasing to the eye, they are a bit more challenging than most other views. Balance and harmony of the elements should be very carefully considered; plan out the placement of your subjects in a sketch to create a feeling of unity in the overall composition.

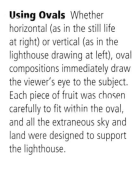

Using Ovals Whether horizontal (as in the still life at right) or vertical (as in the lighthouse drawing at left), oval compositions immediately draw the viewer's eye to the subject. Each piece of fruit was chosen carefully to fit within the oval, and all the extraneous sky and land were designed to support the lighthouse.

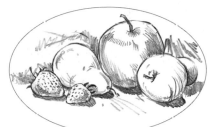

Circular Drawings
A composition with vertical lines, angles, and opposing lines works very well in a circular format, as shown at right. The diagonal lines of the foreground tree limbs, the angle of the stream, and the verticals of the background trees contrast the circle of the picture plane, creating visual interest.

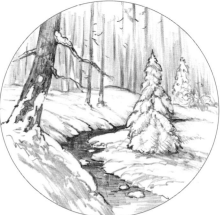

Unique Formats

It is challenging and fun to plan a composition to fit a format that is out of the ordinary, such as the two-part diptych, the three-paneled triptych, the wide panorama, and other extreme-view or unusual formats. The subject of a paneled format must flow smoothly from one panel to another, while maintaining the ability of each panel to stand alone as its own composition. Formats that are either very wide or very tall can accommodate subjects with those special characteristics. And free-form shapes with flowing curves can produce a fluid feeling, leading the eye around a composition. As a practice exercise, select a subject that interests you and create a composition within an unusually shaped format.

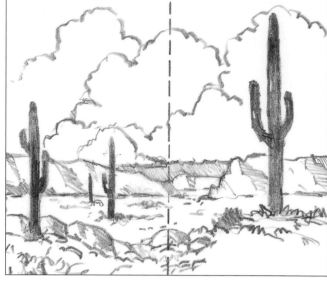

▶ **Diptych** This desert scene can be separated at the dotted line, but the size and placement of the cacti bring the elements together to also function as one composition.

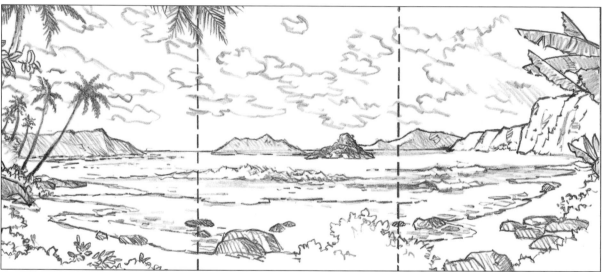

Triptych The foliage on the sides and bottom of this composition provides a scooping frame for the overall design, but each panel of the triptych could stand alone compositionally. Cover any two panels to test this.

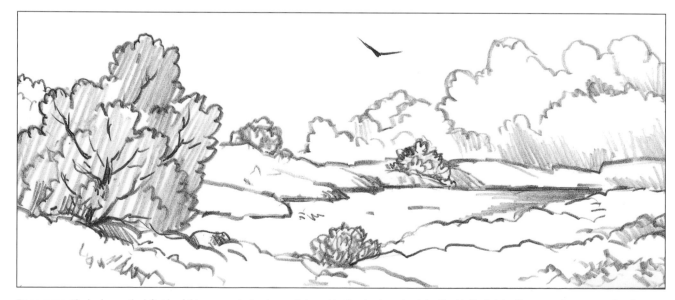

Panorama The bushes on the left side of this panoramic drawing are balanced by the clouds on the right. The bird is slightly off center and acts as a point of interest, bridging the elements on either side and encouraging eye movement.

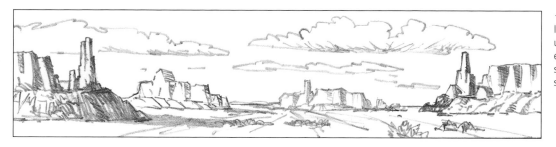

◄ Extreme Horizontal Format The long, horizontal picture plane at left allows us to compose a balanced view of the expansive desert. The vastness of the scene spreading across the exaggerated format seems to surround the viewer.

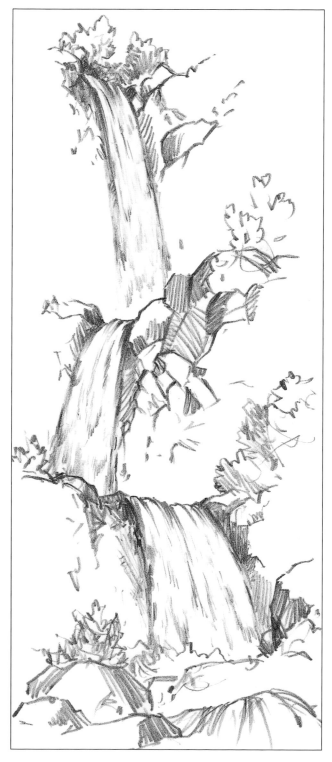

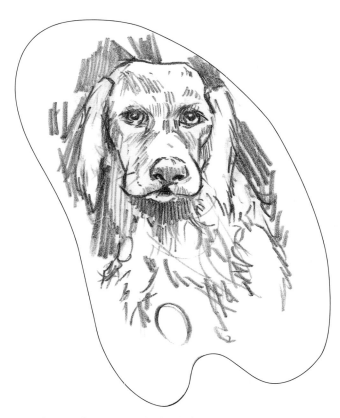

▲ Irregular Format This sketch of a dog on an organically shaped artist's palette creates an interesting and unexpected presentation, which echoes the shape of the animal's head while reflecting the owner's love of art and the pet.

◄ Extreme Vertical Format The waterfall at left has plenty of room to cascade down the tall, narrow picture plane and flow out toward the viewer at the bottom. The surrounding plants and rocks follow the line of the waterfall to heighten the dynamic force of the moving water.

BASIC COMPOSITION METHODS

A successful composition directs the viewer's eye through the drawing, emphasizing the center of interest, or "focal point." Although many factors are involved in creating an effective composition, the way in which you arrange the elements within the drawing is key. We use *value* (lights and darks), *depth* (the illusion of distance or a three-dimensional quality), and *line* (the direction or path the eye follows) to create a natural movement and flow of the elements. There are several basic techniques you can use to achieve an interesting composition; some are based on letters of the alphabet and others are based on forms, shapes, or lines. The diagrams and drawings here illustrate some of these methods.

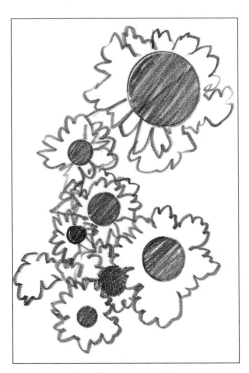

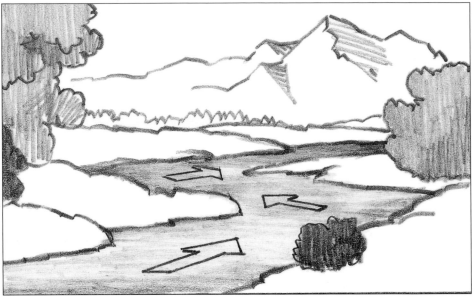

S Shape This composition uses a flattened S shape in the river to lead the viewer into the scene (see arrows). The large tree mass on the left balances the distant mountain and the smaller foliage at the right, pushing the viewer's eye back to the center. At the same time, depth is achieved by varying the light and dark objects in the scene, diminishing the size of distant objects, and using lines delineating the stream that get closer together as they get farther away.

Repetition In this example, one type of flower is repeated in different sizes, which are strategically overlapped to create the composition. The repetition leads the viewer's eye from one flower to the next, largest to smallest and back again, producing smooth eye flow and rhythmic movement throughout the picture plane.

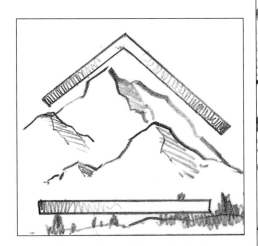

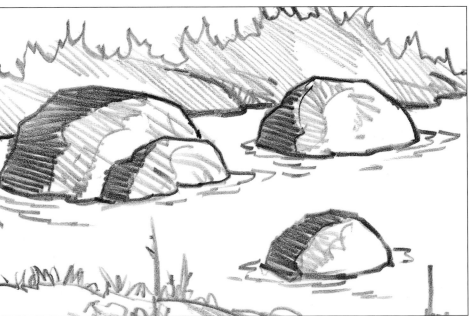

Contrasting Angles and Lines This sketch shows the use of the dramatic, rugged angles of the mountains in contrast with the long, horizontal lines of the ground, which give viewers a calm resting place before their gaze returns to the angular mountains.

Three-Spot Design This common design places three elements in a picture plane in a triangular arrangement to create balance and harmony within the entire scene. Odd numbers keep our eye from pairing off elements and also generate interest. Secondary rocks, shrubs, and water act as supporting elements to the focal rocks.

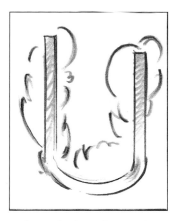

U Shape This shape often is applied as a guide to creating a balanced composition; the curve moves the eye from one side to the other. The U can be distorted by varying the length of the "legs" to achieve a more dynamic effect, as shown here in the foliage height.

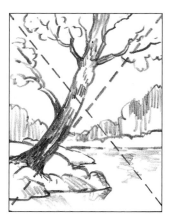

X Shape Here an X is used as the composition guide for a dramatic scene in which the tree almost seems to be falling. The trunk and limbs of the tree form most of the X shape, and the triangle formed by the lake completes it. Other angles echo the basic X design.

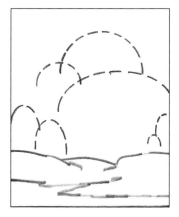

Curved Forms Curved lines are soft and calming. Here the curved forms of the clouds are repeated on the ground as trees or bushes with a similar shape. Diagonal and horizontal lines in the middle ground support and contrast the curved forms, adding interest.

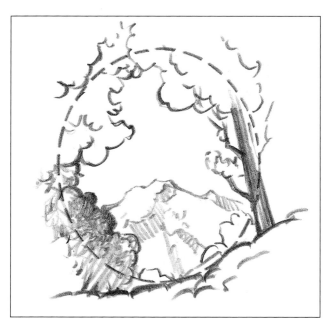

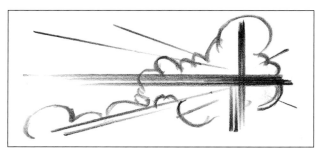

▲ **Cross Shape** The use of a cross shape draws the viewer's attention to the point where the cross members meet, pulling the eye toward the focal point. The cross shape is stable and creates a powerful composition featuring light, as shown here.

◄ **O Shape** To draw the viewer's eye to the center of a composition, place elements around the area in an O shape. Bushes, trees, and foreground foliage are used to form this O, which features the view of the distant mountain.

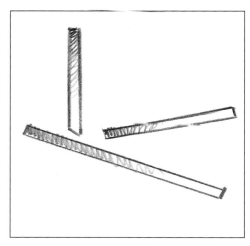

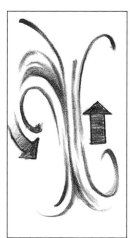

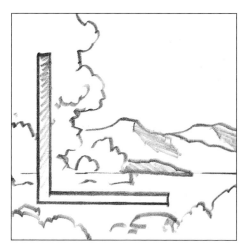

Opposition The sketch on the left uses opposing lines to focus on a point. In the center, a fluid up-and-down movement is achieved by using curved lines to direct the eye. The intersecting lines of the L on the right are formed by the open ground and the tree. When using an L, be careful not to create a scene that is too heavy on one side; balance it with elements on the opposite side.

THE GOLDEN MEAN

The composition of most classical art is based on the Golden Mean, also known as the Golden Ratio, Golden Section, or the Divine Proportion. In ancient Egypt and Greece, design used a constant factor in a geometric progression, and that ratio was first calculated by a mathematician known as Fibonacci in the 13th century. The Golden Mean, or 1.618, is the constant factor in his continued proportion series: 1, 1, 2, 3, 5, 8, 13, 21, 34, 55, 89, 144, and so on. By adding the last number to the previous number, we arrive at the next number in the series; for example, 21 + 34 = 55, 55 + 34 = 89, and so on. By dividing any number by the previous, we get a result close to 1.618. In a continued proportion, the closest pair of numbers to the Golden Mean of 1.618 is 55 and 89—these two numbers are used most frequently in fine design to establish proportionate space.

Finding the Golden Mean in Nature

Examples of the Golden Mean are all around us in nature: the structure of sea shells, leaf and petal groupings, pinecones, pine-apples, and sunflowers, for instance. Several examples are illustrated in the photos on this page. On the following pages, we will work with methods of using the Golden Mean ratio as an organizational tool to determine the optimum size and division of our picture planes.

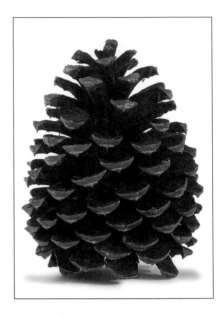

▶ **Naturally Occurring Ratio** The Golden Mean ratio and spiral pattern also can be seen in the structure of most pinecones. Note how the individual pieces spiral up from the bottom of the cone. There actually are two spiral patterns: one to the left and one to the right. Different types of conifers generate different spiral patterns. The pine-apple spirals in this same manner.

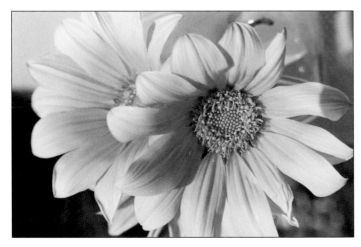

The "Perfect" Ratio of 89:55 The center of the daisy, like the sunflower and other plants with large seed heads, shows the geometric pattern formed by the Golden Ratio. As the seeds or pistils move out from the center of the flower, they create spiral patterns that curve to the right and left at an 89:55 ratio.

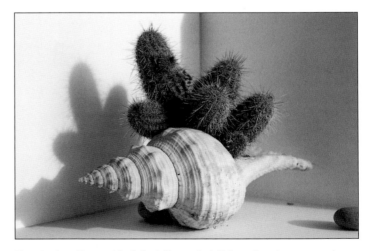

Constant or Geometric Spiral The conch shell shown here demonstrates the Golden Mean—as each section of the spiral naturally increases in size by 1.618 as it moves outward. This is called the "constant spiral" or "geometrical spiral."

Measuring in Units	*The Golden Mean is commonly measured in units based on the perfect ratio. Therefore, as shown in Method 1 on page 61, 2.47 cm would equal 89 units, and 1.53 would equal 55 units (for a total of 144 units).*

Finding the Golden Mean of a Line

The 1:1.618 ratio is used by designers and artists in all media, such as architects, engineers, cabinet makers, and many other creative people. In this exercise, we concentrate on dividing a line into what is commonly accepted as the most aesthetic division.

You can find the Golden Mean of any line by measuring it and using a calculator to divide that number by 1.618 (Method 1). Mark a point at that measurement on the line to divide it into two segments of the perfect proportions. You can continue to divide each smaller section of the line by 1.618 to create more divisions in the Golden Mean ratio. You also can use simple geometry to achieve the same results that the Greeks used in their design (Method 2). Just follow the steps below that illustrate each method.

Method 1: Calculator

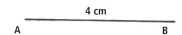

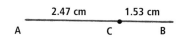

Step 1 Begin by drawing a line of any length and label the two endpoints as A and B. This particular line is 4 cm long.

Step 2 Divide the length (4 cm) by 1.618. The number you get (in this case, 2.47 cm) is the distance between A and C above.

Method 2: Geometry

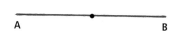

Step 1 Begin by drawing a line of any length and label the two endpoints as A and B. Divide the line length in half and mark the center point.

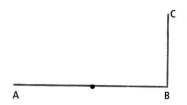

Step 2 Draw a perpendicular line at point B that is equal in length to half of line AB (the measurement from the center point to A or B). Label the end of the new line point C (BC = 1/2 AB).

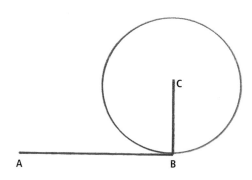

Step 3 Draw a circle with the center at point C and BC as the radius.

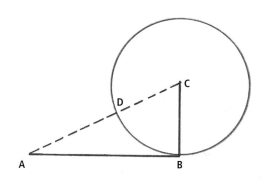

Step 4 Draw a line from A to C. Label the point where line AC passes through the circle as point D.

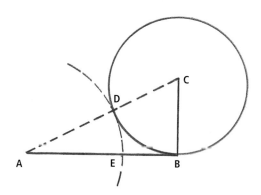

Step 5 Using point A as the center and AD as the radius, draw a partial circle which intersects line AB; that intersection is at point E (EA = AD). You should find that line AE equals a division of 144/89 and line EB equals a division of 89/55, where 144 is the original line length (AB). Contrast is created by the differing sizes of lines AE and EB, and unity is created by the correlation of line EB to the entire line AB (the Golden Mean).

Creating a Golden Mean Rectangle

The square and the rectangle are two of the most important picture planes for two-dimensional art compositions. Infinite numbers of width and length combinations for these areas exist, but none are more pleasing to the eye and aesthetically proportioned than the Golden Mean rectangle. This rectangle is based upon the same ancient rules of aesthetic proportion used by the Greeks in their art and architecture. There are several approaches to creating a rectangle that conforms to the Golden Mean proportions. The following is one method explained in four simple steps.

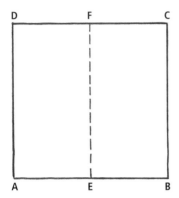

Step 1 Draw a perfect square (ABCD), which will serve as the base for all measurements when creating your Golden Mean rectangle. The length of AD should be the length you want for the short side of your rectangle when it is finished. Divide AB in half to find E, and divide DC in half to find F; then draw a vertical center line (EF) through the square.

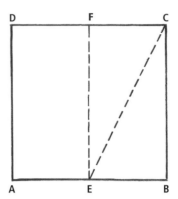

Step 2 Next draw a line from point E (the halfway mark on the line AB) on a diagonal up to the right corner of the square (C). This line (EC) becomes the basis for the length of the rectangle extension. Set your drawing compass to the length of EC as its radius or measure the length with your ruler.

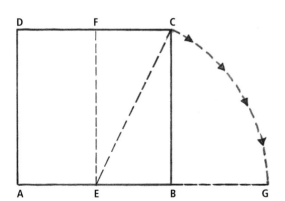

Step 3 Use the compass or ruler to drop the diagonal line (EC) down until it becomes horizontal, on the same line with A, E, and B. Line EG = EC and BG is the extension length which will create the Golden Mean rectangle. The sides of the rectangle (AD and AG) are in proportion at the 1:1.618 ratio.

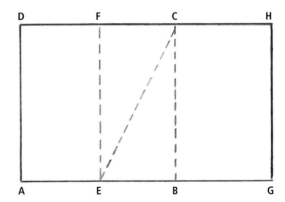

Step 4 Draw lines to complete the rectangle, from B to G, G to H, and C to H. Notice the "ghost" lines that indicate the steps taken to construct a true Golden Mean rectangle. The ratios of 55:89 and 1:1.618 apply to the areas of the original square as compared to the complete rectangle.

Spiral Patterns in Compositions

Down through the centuries, scientists and artists alike have employed the Golden Mean in their work. Leonardo da Vinci used the Golden Mean extensively in his drawings and inventions. Archimedes—a mathematician, engineer, and inventor who lived in ancient Greece—is famous for his work in physics, which involves focusing on circles, spheres, and cylinders. His theories of spirals are based on a plane curve moving away from or toward a center point at a constant rate. By definition, a two-dimensional *spiral* is a line winding around a center point while continuously moving away from or toward it.

Using Archimedes' principles, the Golden Mean rectangle created on the previous page can be further divided, and a natural spiral can be created within it, using curves drawn on the radius of the square within the rectangle (see instructions below). If you rotate your paper 1/4 turn counter-clockwise each time you draw a curve, you easily can see where to work next. Always divide the new, rectangular section of the Golden Mean rectangle using the length of the shorter side of the new section to mark off the square in that section and drawing a new quarter circle within it. Each curved line is drawn with the radius of the square it is in and connects to the one before it to form the spiral.

There are a variety of spiral patterns in nature, and many of them fall into the pattern of an Archimedean spiral (see page 60 for examples). To create the gentle spiral we see in the conch shell, follow the instructions below.

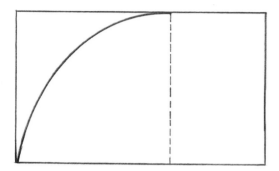

Step 1 Draw a Golden Mean rectangle as we did on the previous page. Erase the extra lines but not the side of the square (BC). Next, draw a 1/4-circle curve in the square with the length of the side as its radius and positioned as shown above.

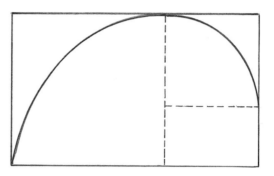

Step 2 Divide the smaller portion of the rectangle (on the right) into another Golden Mean proportion, drawing a square within it using the length of the shorter side of the rectangle as the length of the sides of the square. Continue the curve as shown.

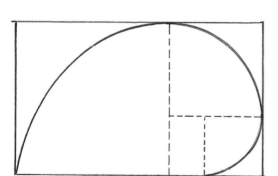

Step 3 Divide the smaller portion of that rectangle into another Golden Mean proportion. Draw a second square using the shorter side of the rectangle as the length for the sides of the square. Continue the curve with the new radius, as shown.

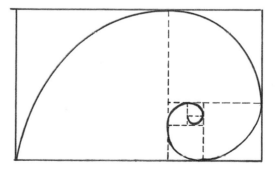

Step 4 Continue dividing each smaller rectangular proportion and drawing the gentle curve in the square as before. This progression can be repeated until you have reached the immediate center point from which the curve originates, if desired.

DIVIDING THE PICTURE PLANE

In addition to the Golden Mean, many other methods can be used to divide the picture plane into a pleasing and balanced composition and help with the placement of elements. The *rule of thirds,* for instance, is accomplished by drawing lines that divide the picture plane into thirds, both vertically and horizontally, to form a grid that is used as a guide for placing elements. Some artists call it a simplified Golden Mean rectangle, but it is not, because these thirds do not fall into the perfect ratio of 1:1.618.

Once you have the grid of thirds established on the picture plane, it can be further divided within itself to create even more complexity in the composition. The intersections of the grid lines are excellent points for placing objects (rather than drawing them in the direct center of that space). Other methods of dividing the plane use diagonals and right angles; some methods are illustrated here in the small, thumbnail diagrams with the larger drawings beside them. All of the examples are shown using a Golden Mean rectangle as the picture plane, but they also can be applied to other formats.

▶ **Basic Rule of Thirds** This diagram shows the basic rule-of-thirds division and object placement. The large, rounded vase in the drawing sits on the lower left grid point and the flowers in the vase sit on the upper left grid point. The two smaller flowers and the line of the drapery balance the composition with their corresponding placement at the right points of the grid; they also lead the viewer's eye back to the arrangement.

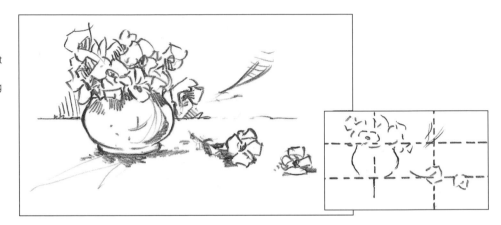

◀ **Thirds with One Diagonal** Here the rule of thirds is used with a diagonal. Grid lines divide the plane into three equal parts, vertically and horizontally. The pine tree is aligned on the left vertical with its trunk ending on the lower left grid point. The mountain peak falls on the upper right grid point, and a diagonal between the two assists in moving the viewer's eye down to the tree.

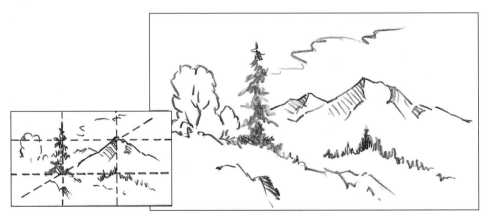

▶ **Thirds with Two Diagonals** The rule of thirds also can be applied by drawing a diagonal line from one corner to the other. Then lines at 90° to the diagonal extend to the corners. Horizontal and vertical grid lines can then be placed at the intersections of the lines. This forms a grid of thirds with a larger central area and also creates pathways for placing elements like the mountains and the tree line.

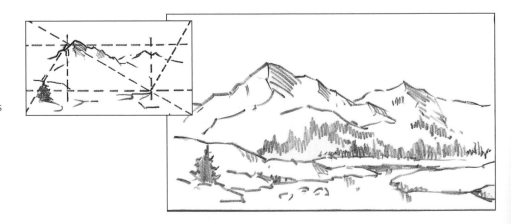

▶ **Horizontal Division** This simple method of division helps us avoid placing the horizon or any other important horizontal element directly on the center line of the picture plane. The scene is divided into three major parts: background, middle ground, and foreground. Elements in each of those areas—the birds, waves, foam, and rocks—contrast the primarily horizontal orientation of the scene.

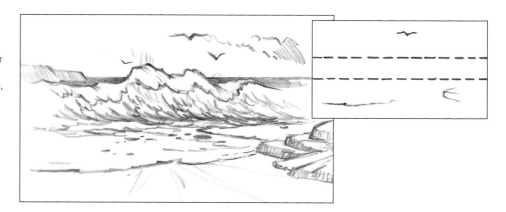

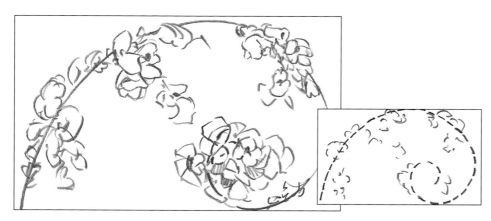

◀ **Golden Mean Spiral** Formed using the method on the page 63, the spiral created in a Golden Mean rectangle is a wonderful guide for graceful floral designs and even landscapes. This spiral can be rotated on the picture plane or reduced in size. If you wish, you can use only a portion of the spiral or combine a spiral with one of the other division methods.

▶ **Diagonal with Opposition** Simply draw a diagonal line across the picture plane; then draw a line at 90° to the diagonal extending to a corner, as shown. The focal point should be placed where the two lines meet. In this drawing, a weathered tree is placed there; the line of the middle-ground hills runs along the diagonal to lead the viewer's eye to the tree.

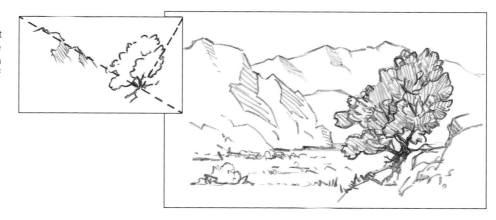

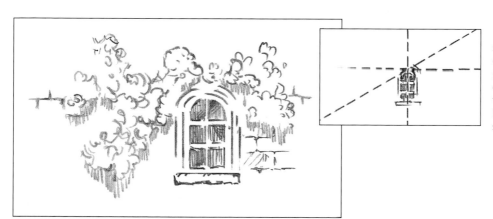

◀ **Off-Center Division** To place elements just slightly off center like this window and greenery, draw a vertical line in the area where you think the primary subject should be placed (avoiding the center of the paper). Then draw a diagonal line from corner to corner. Add a horizontal line where the first two lines cross. This line is a perfect guide for placing secondary elements, like the vines here.

SYMMETRY AND ASYMMETRY

Symmetry is the balanced similarity of form on either side of a dividing line. *Asymmetry* is the lack of symmetry. Two common types of symmetry are bilateral and radial. *Bilateral* or *mirror* symmetry occurs when the right and left sides or top and bottom of an element or composition are counterparts to one another, such as our bodies, most fruit, and the letters A, B, and H. In *radial* symmetry, similar parts are evenly arranged around a central point, as in a starfish or snowflakes. Symmetry can apply to both geometric and natural patterns and shapes.

Symmetry and asymmetry in a composition can be seen in the individual elements and in their relationship to each other. Generally, asymmetry in compositions is more interesting than symmetry, which can be monotonous and fail to capture the viewer's interest. A combination of symmetry and asymmetry makes a composition compelling to the viewer.

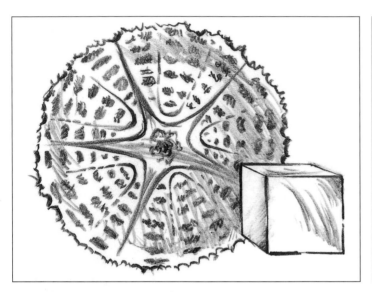

Radial Symmetry A sea urchin has five sets of plates that are arranged symmetrically around an axis at the base. A salt crystal is an example of three-dimensional symmetry with all the surfaces equidistant from the center.

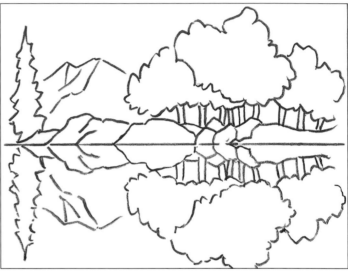

Mirror Symmetry A landscape scene like this one can be "mirrored" or repeated upside down in still water. If there were movement on the water's surface, the reflection would be distorted and the composition would be less symmetrical.

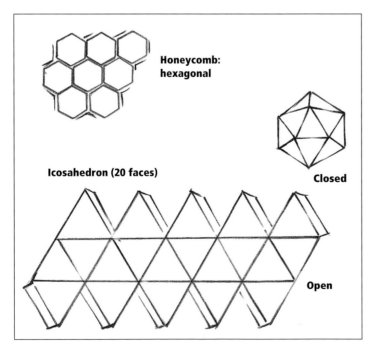

Geometrical Symmetry A honeycomb has a naturally precise hexagonal pattern of repeating symmetry. An icosahedron, carefully drawn with 20 triangular faces, is pictured open and closed to show its symmetry.

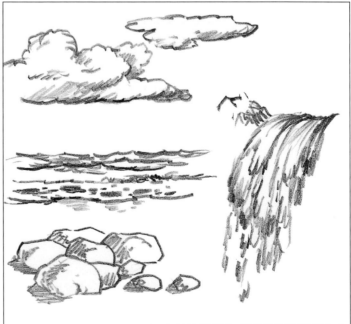

Non-Geometrical Symmetry The natural elements above have been used for centuries in basic design. Although not absolutely symmetrical, they suggest symmetry through repetition of shape and line and balance of weight.

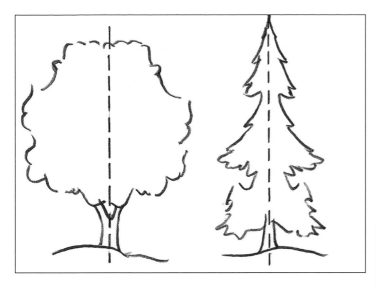

◀ **Bilateral Symmetry** These trees are exactly alike on both sides of the dividing line. Such shapes rarely occur in nature and present an unnatural look within a landscape composition. Precise symmetry is rarely used in successful compositions.

▶ **Bilateral Asymmetry** Here are the same two trees as shown above, but these have been drawn with slightly different sides. This asymmetry makes the trees appear more natural and realistic; our eye actually sees this as a more appealing image. This is a good example of appropriate use of asymmetry in a composition.

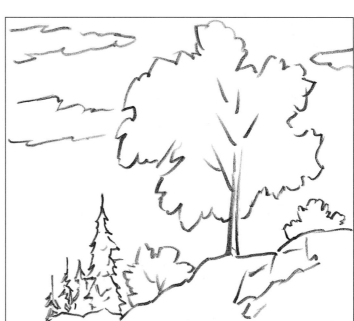

◀ **Symmetrical Placement** The basically symmetrical form and placement of the pine trees is dominant, balanced by the asymmetrical shapes of the broadleaf trees, mountain, and clouds. This composition shows the use of "translatory symmetry," an element repeated to direct the eye into the distance.

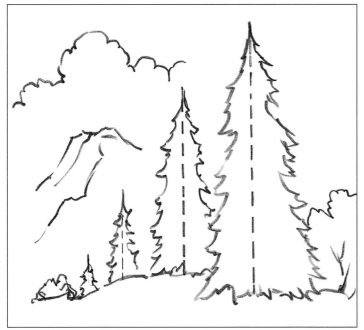

▶ **Asymmetrical Placement** The rounded asymmetry of the large, broadleaf tree in the foreground on the diagonal horizon line is dominant, balanced by the placement of the pines and the horizontal floating clouds. This composition is based on the "Contrasting Angles and Lines" method (see 58).

USING VALUES

Now that we have looked at methods for dividing the picture plane and considered the use of line and placement of the elements, we need to focus on the impact of value on our compositions. As you learned in Chapter 1, values are the light to dark shadings in our drawings that give our compositions a lifelike depiction of depth. The viewer's eye is naturally drawn to areas of great contrast between values—where the darkest darks meet the lightest lights. We intentionally place values in our compositions to help direct the viewer's eye to the most important areas of our drawings. These values also can help set the mood of your composition. The three drawings here illustrate different ways you can use value as a compositional element.

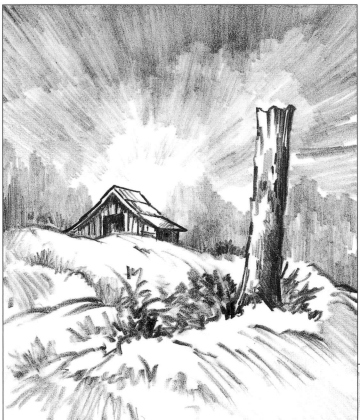

◄ **Directional Value Rendering** In this example, the values in this sunset sky range from the bright highlight of the setting sun to the dark sky behind the clouds. The background values of the sky are made with radiating strokes that seem to converge at one point in the middle ground, lightening in value as they near the center. This dramatic effect is built through lines of varying values that lead the viewer's eye to the barn. These lines are contrasted by middle-value, vertical strokes in the background trees. Note that all foreground shading and lines lead to the center of the composition for emphasis.

▶ **Minimal Use of Values** This scene uses dark values to make the leafless tree the focal point of the composition; other elements are in a narrow range of light to middle values, so they don't draw attention away from the tree. The direction of the clouds is established with middle-value lines that lead back to the ground. The middle ground and foreground are developed using limited range of values, again to keep the focus on the barren tree. The dark values of the foliage and the fence posts keep the eye circulating around the composition, but there isn't enough contrast to create any confusion about the focal point. By using minimal values and keeping the elements simple, you can make a powerful statement when creating a focal element.

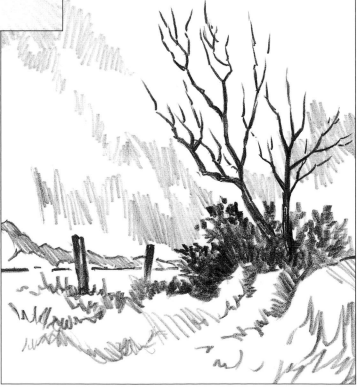

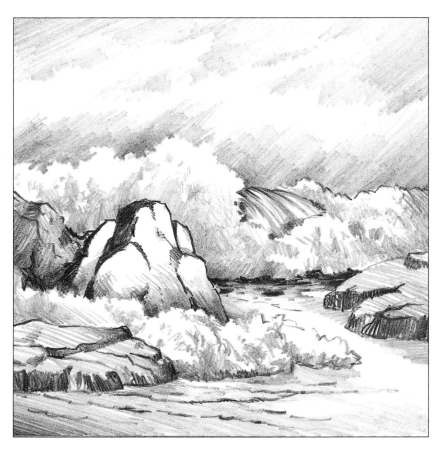

◀ Maximum Value Range

This composition has three horizontal divisions: background; foreground; and middle ground, which shows the greatest range of values. The lightest values emphasize the most important elements—the middle-ground boulder and breaking wave; the light areas are contrasted with adjacent dark shading to draw the viewer's attention to these elements. The foam and water are shaded with smooth but lightly textured hatching (parallel lines) and crosshatching (overlapping sets of parallel lines at different angles). The edge of the wave where it strikes the rocks is emphasized by the shading beneath it. The diagonal shading of the sky balances the opposite action of the waves and movement of the water.

▶ **Value Sketch** To render a drawing with a wide range of values, begin by developing a small value-pattern sketch like the one at right, which shows the main subjects and preliminary shading. As you see the areas develop in the sketch, you can move, lighten, or darken values to enhance the statement of the work. Then use this sketch as a guide for your final drawing, which will show more detail and a wider range of values.

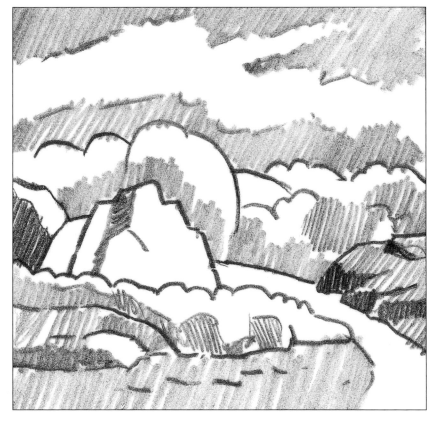

CREATING A FOCAL POINT

A key element in creating a successful composition is including more than one area of interest, without generating confusion about the subject of the drawing. Compositions are often based on one large object, which is balanced by the grouping, placement, and values of smaller objects. Directing the viewer's eye with secondary focal points helps move the viewer through a scene, so that it can be enjoyed in its entirety.

The primary focal point should immediately capture the viewer's attention through size, line quality, value, placement on the picture plane, and the proximity of other points of interest which call attention to it. The secondary focal point is the area that the eye naturally moves to after seeing the primary focal point; usually this element is a smaller object or objects with less detail. Another secondary focal point may be at some distance from the viewer's eye, appearing much smaller, and showing only minor detailing, so that it occupies a much less important space in the drawing. This distant focal point serves to give the viewer's eye another stop on the journey around the composition before returning to the primary focal point.

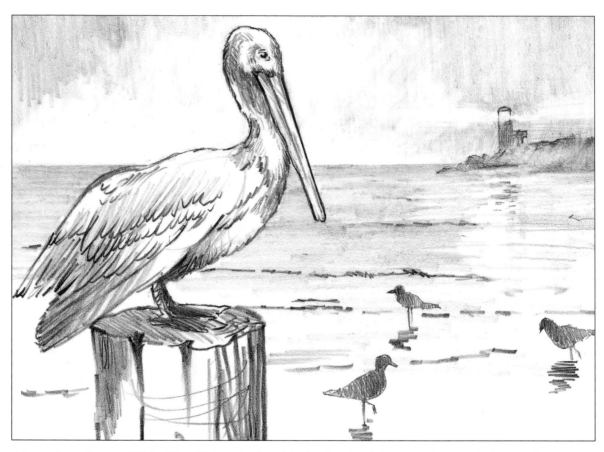

Primary, Secondary, and Distant Focal Points The size and detail on the pelican designates it as the primary focal point, and it immediately catches the viewer's eye. The pelican's gaze and the point of its bill shifts the attention to the small birds in the foreground (the secondary focal point). By keeping the texture and value changes subtle in the middle ground, the eye moves freely to this point. These three small birds are shaded fairly evenly so they don't detract from the primary focal point. The triangle created by the birds, along with the water's edge and the point of land, leads the viewer's eye to another, more distant focal point—the lighthouse. Here the two subtle rays of light against the shaded background suggest a visual path. The rays of light, the point of land, and the horizon line all work together to bring the viewer's eye back to the pelican, and the visual journey begins again.

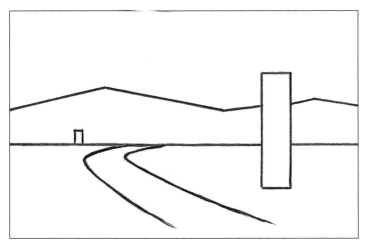

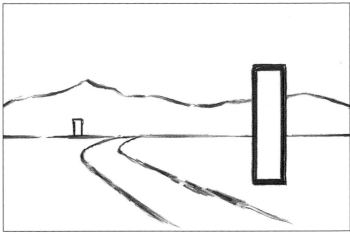

Lack of Focal Point When all lines in a composition are drawn with the same depth of intensity (value) and width, the entire design appears flat and uninteresting, with no focal point.

Focal Depth and Flow By simply changing the weight of the lines of the foreground rectangle, and by varying the quality of lines in the road and mountain, the scene has more focal interest.

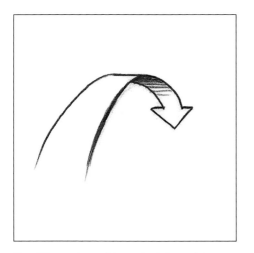

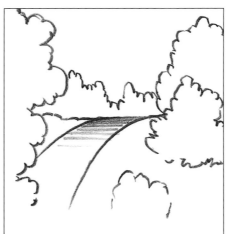

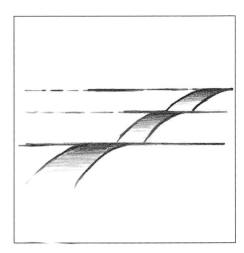

Focal Curve A graceful curve leads the eye into the composition. This can be used for roads and pathways to create the illusion of hills and valleys, and also in subjects like floral arrangements to direct the viewer's eye.

Focal Depth The focal curve is one way of creating depth in a composition; here it serves as a road in a natural setting, leading the viewer into the scene. The use of overlapping elements—the trees—also adds to the illusion, creating focal depth.

Multiple Focal Curves To further accentuate the feeling of distance, more than one curve can be used, along with multiple elevation lines. Notice that the curve segments are displaced and become smaller as they recede in the distance.

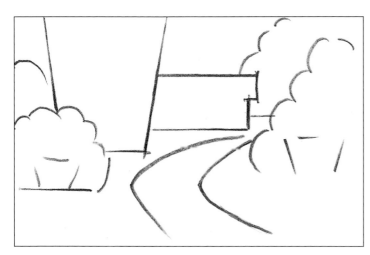

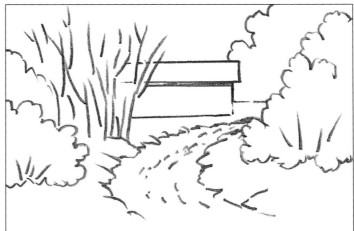

Sketching Focal Patterns Sketch a preliminary, simple pattern plan to show the general placement of elements without the distraction of internal details, value or line quality. Look for the focal pattern—how the eye moves around the picture and what is important—and adjust as needed.

Develop the Pattern After sketching and adjusting a preliminary pattern plan, lightly add details to build the feeling of rhythmic movement and depth. Begin varying the weight of the lines and refining the shapes of the elements. As you continue, use value to further accentuate the focal pattern.

FORMING AND PLACING ELEMENTS

The basic shapes used in creating visual art—the square, rectangle, circle, and triangle—are two-dimensional (2-D). The diagrams below show how to create the illusion of depth (three dimensions or 3-D) by extending each 2-D shape. These 3-D forms are combined and modified to form the elements we draw. For an effective composition, they must be overlapped on the picture plane to unify the elements and provide depth. At the same time, the arrangement must display balance in which the elements' size, placement, and value occupy the space to create a harmonious composition.

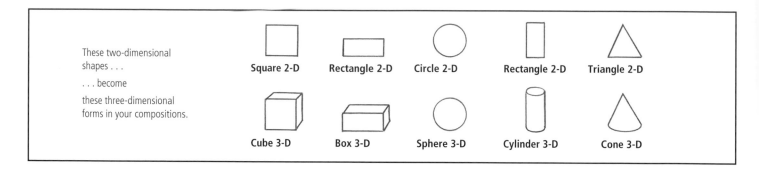

These two-dimensional shapes . . .

. . . become

these three-dimensional forms in your compositions.

| Square 2-D | Rectangle 2-D | Circle 2-D | Rectangle 2-D | Triangle 2-D |
| Cube 3-D | Box 3-D | Sphere 3-D | Cylinder 3-D | Cone 3-D |

Arranging Elements in a Still Life

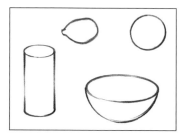

Turning Shape into Form Derived from basic shapes, these elements can be used in a still life composition. Cut a sphere in half for a bowl. A circle can become an orange; a cylinder, a can. Stretch a circle horizontally to create a lemonlike ellipse.

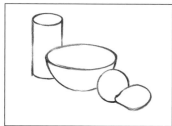

Monotonous Composition Placing the elements in a continuous line, as shown here, creates monotony and boredom. There is a slight sense of depth achieved by overlapping, but all the attention is focused on the last item, the vertical can.

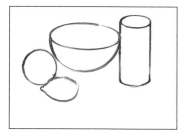

No Depth or Balance This C-shaped composition offers a slightly better placement, but when elements are just touching—not overlapping—nothing creates depth or balance.

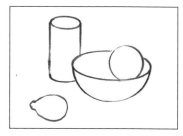

Pleasing Composition Here some elements overlap—the orange is placed in the bowl for further interest. The elements balance one another and hold the viewer's interest.

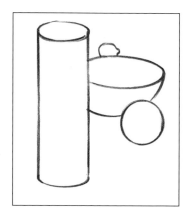

One Dominant Element This arrangement is fairly comfortable, even though the cylinder is quite dominant. If you wish to emphasize one major element, be sure that it is worthy of the attention and that the other elements support it. Overlapping the objects creates depth and supports the cylinder.

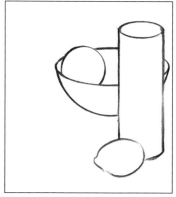

Unbalanced Placement Even though all these objects are overlapping and the orange is once again placed in the bowl for interest, the viewer is left with the feeling that everything is falling off the page. In addition, the side of the cylinder is at the center of the bowl, visually cutting the composition in half.

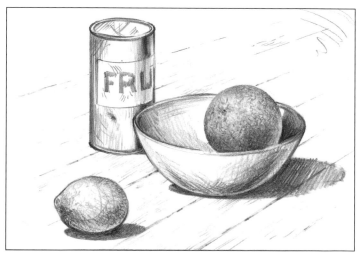

Placing Still Life Elements This finished sketch uses the "Pleasing Composition" thumbnail above as a guide. The two-dimensional shapes of the thumbnail have been transformed into three-dimensional forms through shading to create highlights, shadows, textures, and a surface (the wooden table). The finished composition shows depth and dimension.

ARRANGING A FLORAL COMPOSITION

Few drawing subjects require more intensive composition than a floral arrangement, which is a work of art in its own right. Carefully consider balance, line, value, and form, and limit the number of flowers so each can be seen and appreciated. An even number of elements can make a very balanced floral composition, but avoid arranging the flowers so that they visually "pair up," as this stops the viewer's eye. For that reason, many artists prefer to group flowers in odd numbers or arrange them so that they form a triangle. Often the leaves become as important as the flowers themselves; limit the amount of greenery to allow the flowers to be the primary focal point. Likewise, the choice of vase or other container to hold the flowers should be complementary to the floral type: for example, an informal bunch of daisies might look fine in a basket. Even the drapery beneath and behind the floral arrangement has an impact on the statement the composition makes. Follow this step-by-step rendering which illustrates these points.

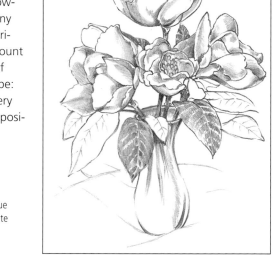

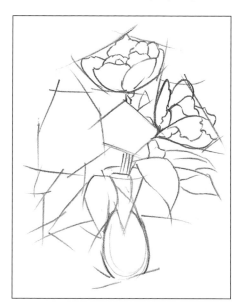

▶ **Step 3** Begin shading and concentrate on value changes in each segment as shapes overlap to create depth.

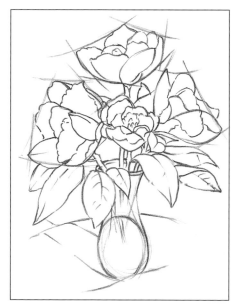

▲ **Step 1** Block in the magnolias and large leaves to form a triangle, which mirrors the cone-shaped top of the vase.

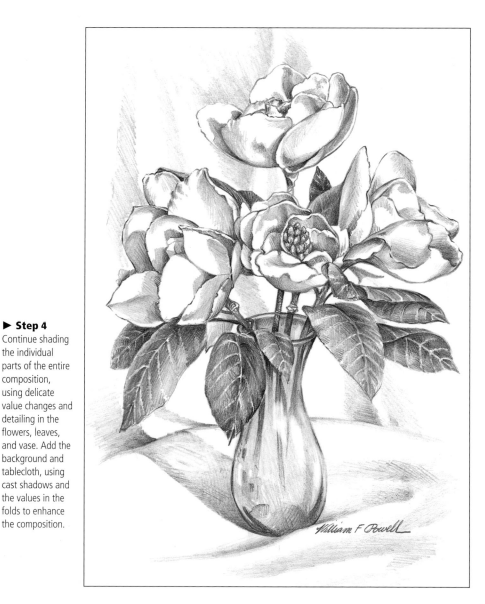

▶ **Step 4** Continue shading the individual parts of the entire composition, using delicate value changes and detailing in the flowers, leaves, and vase. Add the background and tablecloth, using cast shadows and the values in the folds to enhance the composition.

▲ **Step 2** Refine the lines, letting the curve of the leaves lead the eye down to the vase and then up the stems to the flowers.

PLACING PEOPLE IN A COMPOSITION

The positioning and size of a person on the picture plane is of utmost importance to the composition. The open or "negative" space around the portrait subject generally should be larger than the area occupied by the subject, providing a sort of personal space surrounding them. Whether you are drawing only the face, a head-and-shoulders portrait, or a complete figure, thoughtful positioning will establish a pleasing composition with proper balance. Practice drawing thumbnail sketches of people to study the importance of size and positioning.

Basics of Portraiture

Correct placement on the picture plane is key to a good portrait, and the eyes of the subject are the key to placement. The eyes catch the viewer's attention first, so they should not be placed on either the horizontal or vertical center line of the picture plane; preferably, the eyes should be placed above the center line. Avoid drawing too near the sides, top, or bottom of the picture plane, as this gives an uneasy feeling of imbalance.

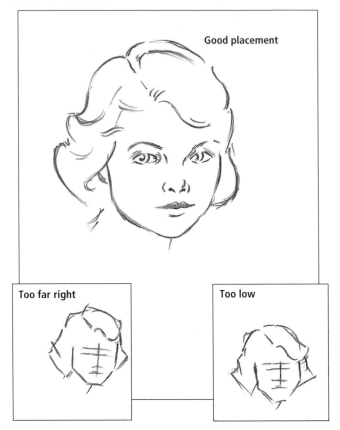

Good placement

Too far right

Too low

▶ **Placement of a Portrait** The smaller thumbnails here show the girl's head placed too far to the side and too low in the picture plane, suggesting that she might "slide off" the page. The larger sketch shows the face at a comfortable and balanced horizontal and vertical position, which allows room to add an additional element of interest to enhance the composition.

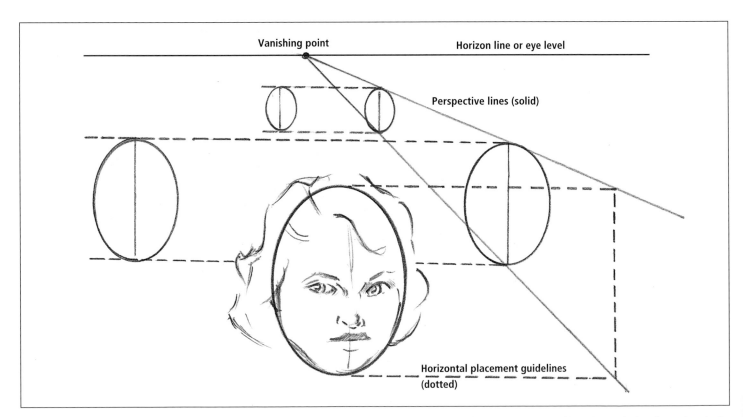

Vanishing point

Horizon line or eye level

Perspective lines (solid)

Horizontal placement guidelines (dotted)

Multiple Subjects If you are drawing several, similarly sized subjects, use the rules of perspective to determine relative size. Draw a vanishing point on a horizon line and a pair of perspective lines. Receding guidelines extended from the perspective lines will indicate the top of the head and chin of faces throughout the composition. The heads become smaller as they get farther from the viewer.

Adding Elements to Portraits

Many portraits are drawn without backgrounds to avoid distracting the viewer from the subject. If you do add background elements to portraits, be sure to control the size, shape, and arrangement of elements surrounding the figure. Additions should express the personality or interests of the subject.

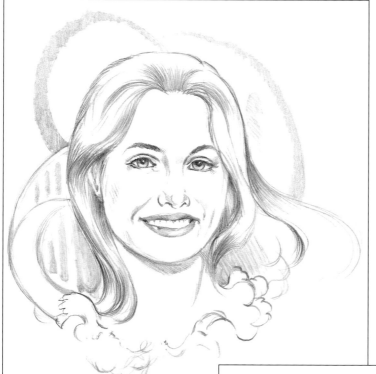

◄ Repetition of Shapes within the Portrait
The delicate features of this young woman are emphasized by the simple, abstract elements in the background. The flowing curves fill much of the negative space, while accenting the elegance of the woman's hair and features. Simplicity of form is important in this composition; the portrait highlights only her head and neck. Notice that her eyes meet the eyes of the viewer—a dramatic and compelling feature.

▼ Depicting the Subject's Interest This portrait of a young man includes a background that shows his interest in rocketry. The straight lines in the back-ground contrast the rounded shapes of the human form. Although the back-ground detail is complex, it visually recedes and serves to balance the man's weight. The focus remains on the man, but we've generated visual interest by adding elements to the composition.

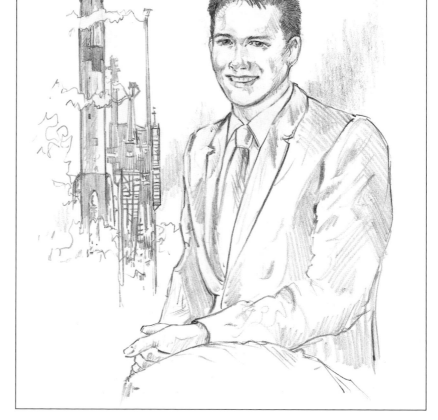

TIP

Using a photo of a friend or relative, experiment with adding varied backgrounds. See how each choice can change the mood and appearance of that portrait.

Adding Complete Figures

Creating a composition that shows a complete person can be challenging. A standing figure is much taller than it is wide, so the figure should be positioned so that its action relates naturally to the eye level of the viewer and the horizon line.

   To place more than one figure on the picture plane, use perspective as we did with the portrait heads. Remember that people appear smaller and less distinct when they are more distant. For comfortable placement of people in a composition, they should be on the same eye level as the viewer with the horizon line about waist high.

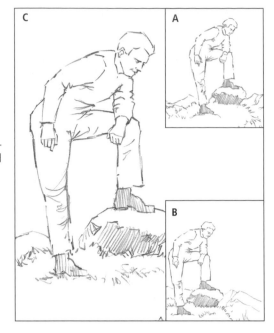

▶ **Full Figure Placement** In thumbnail A, the subject is too perfectly centered in the picture plane. In thumbnail B, the figure is placed too far to the left. Thumbnail C is an example of effective placement of a human figure in a composition.

◀ **Sizing Multiple Figures** For realistic compositions, we need to keep figures in proportion. All the figures here are in proportion; we use perspective to determine the height of each figure. Start by drawing a horizon line and placing a vanishing point on it. Then draw your main character (on the right here) to which all others will be proportional. Add light perspective lines from the top and bottom of the figure to the vanishing point to determine the height of other figures. If we want figures on the other side of the vanishing point, we draw horizontal placement guidelines from the perspective lines to determine his height, and then add perspective lines on that side.

▶ **Line of Sight** Figures in a composition like this one can relate to each other or to objects within the scene through line of sight (shown here as dotted lines). You can show line of sight with the eyes, but also by using head position and even a pointing hand. These indications can guide the viewer to a particular point of interest in the composition. Though the man on the left is facing forward, his eyes are looking to our right. The viewer's eye follows the line of sight of those within the drawing and is guided around the picture plane as the people interact. The man at the top is looking straight up.

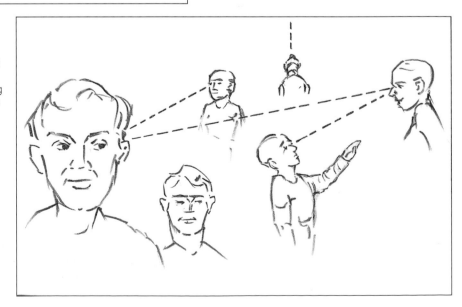

Placement of Single and Grouped Figures

Artists often use the external shape and mass of figures to assist in placing elements within a composition—individual figures form various geometric shapes based on their pose and several figures in close proximity form one mass. Establish a concept of what you want to show in your composition, and make thumbnail studies before attempting the final drawing. The following exercise is based on using the shape and mass of single and grouped figures to create the drawing at the bottom of the page.

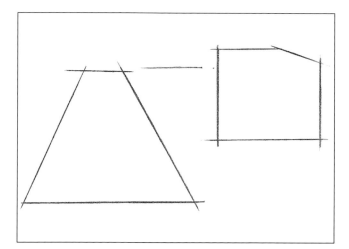

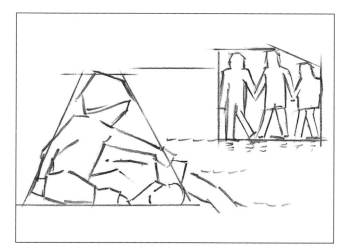

Step 1 Begin by considering the overall setting—foreground, middle ground, and background—for a subject like these children at the beach. You can use elements from different photos and place them in one setting. Block in the basic shapes of your subjects; the boy in the foreground is a clipped triangular shape, and the group of children forms a rough rectangle. Determine balanced placement of the two masses of people.

Step 2 Next, sketch in outlines of the figures. The little boy with the shovel and pail occupies an area close to the viewer. The three children occupy a slightly smaller mass in the middle ground at the water's edge. Even though there are three children in this area, they balance the little boy through size and placement at the opposite corner. The wave and water line unite the composition and lead the eye between the two masses.

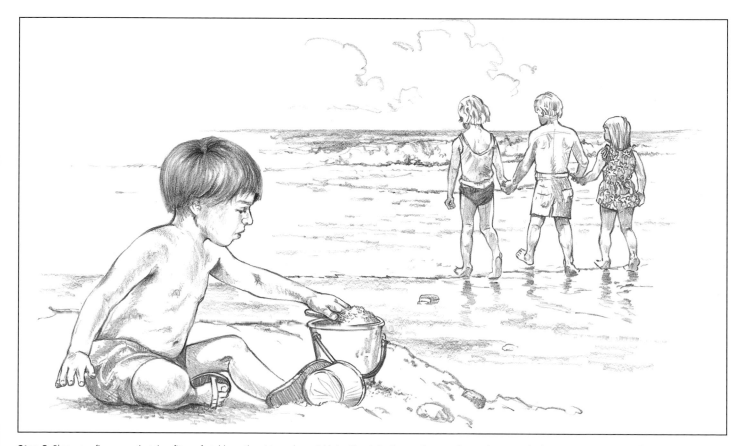

Step 3 Place your figures so that they fit comfortably on the picture plane. Add detail and shading to elements that are important in the composition. Use an element in the foreground to help direct the viewer's eye to other areas, such as the outstretched arm of the boy. Placing the small rock between the middle- and foreground creates a visual stepping stone to the three children at right.

COMPOSING LANDSCAPES

When you are composing a landscape, consider the elements you want to include and adjust their size, placement, values, and lines to create a pleasing and balanced composition. The following examples show the relationship of basic elements to one another and to the picture plane in a landscape. The lines could represent trees, buildings, flowers, or other elements in a composition.

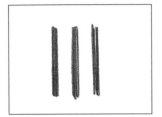 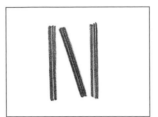 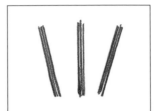 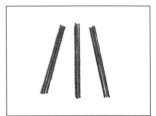

Too Uniform When objects are all uniform, centered on the picture plane, and absolutely balanced, the composition can be monotonous.

Some Interest Angling the object in the center creates interest, but this design is still too uniform; it doesn't lead the eye through the composition.

Too Much Opposition These elements have balanced placement, but the outward angle of the side elements gives an unsettling feeling.

Unsteadiness Although this arrangement is secure and balanced, it still imparts a feeling of unsteadiness. Less severe angles might help.

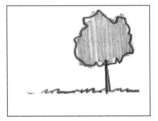 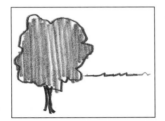 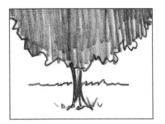 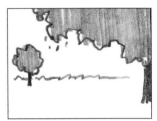

Unbalanced The tree is not balanced by any other object on the picture plane, which makes it seem uninteresting and isolated.

Uncomfortable The tree is the sole focus. It is too far forward and too far to the left for a balanced placement.

Overpowering The tree overwhelms the picture plane, dividing it in half. There's nowhere for the viewer's eye to move.

Comfortable The tree at right is partially out of the picture plane. Its leaves lead the viewer's eye to the small tree.

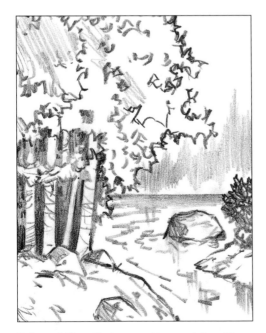

Balanced Mass The foreground trees are balanced by the rock, land, and bush to the right, with the lake and background trees for support.

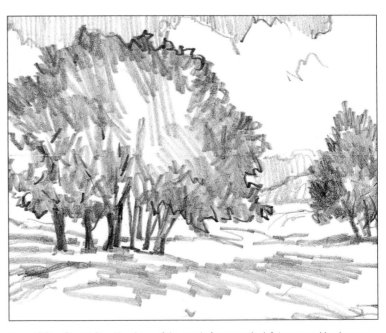

Repetition for Unity The shape of the stand of trees on the left is repeated by the more distant grouping on the right. The curve of the clouds echoes the tree shapes and hills, which also helps to unify the composition.

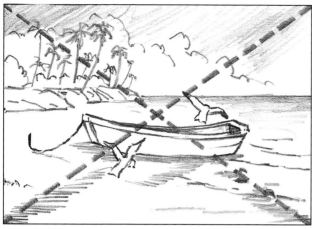

◄ X-Shaped Composition In the drawings at left and below, notice the division of background, middle ground, and foreground. Elements and values are placed within the picture plane in an X shape. Distant palms angle downward toward the boat and the seagulls are moving toward the upper right. Variations in shading create the feeling of depth in the scene. Placing the boat horizontally in the foreground just below and to the right of the X-marked center of the picture plane holds the eye, identifying the boat as the main focal point.

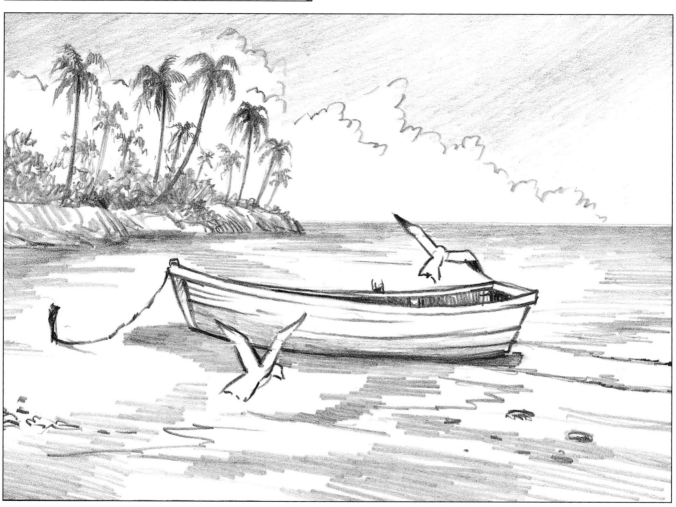

Variation of Focal Element Draw the scene above, substituting each of the boats shown below. Changing the focal element will alter the composition dramatically, leading the eye to different areas of the drawing.

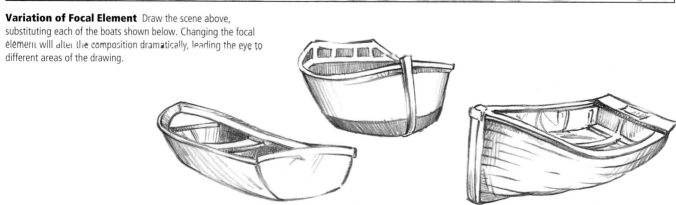

USING NEGATIVE SPACE

Negative space is the area of a composition that is around or between the focal elements. Often this negative space is as important to the composition as the focal elements, providing balance and unity. Observing and drawing the details within the negative space—even before completing the other elements—is an important technique in creating a realistic composition. The negative space supports the focal elements by offering both repetition and contrast in line, values, textures, and shapes to heighten interest in the composition.

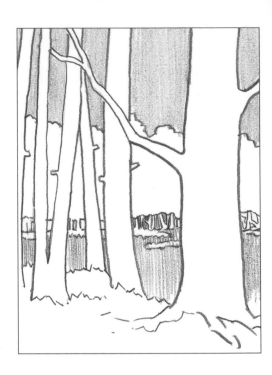

▶ **Blocking in Negative Spaces** In this sketch, everything between the foreground trees is negative space. Use light guidelines to define the large tree trunks. For interest, contrast those strong verticals with the horizontals that form the sky, foliage, and open middle ground, creating a pleasing composition. Begin to add the shading within those negative spaces.

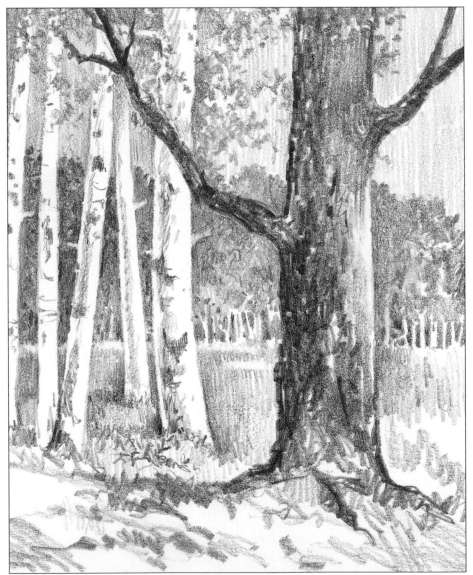

◀ **Adding Details for a Balanced Composition**
Now we add details within the negative shapes to give the composition depth, contrast, and balance. Notice that the white-barked birch trees are defined by the darks in the negative space around them; their area is balanced by that darker area of foliage behind them. The deeply shaded, heavily textured tree in the foreground is balanced by the lighter, smoother area of the sky; the value of the vertical dark strokes on the tree should be highly controlled to create an element of major importance without causing the eye to struggle to see the rest of the scene. Foreground grass strokes and details should be soft and supportive to the scene without catching the eye and disrupting the carefully balanced composition.

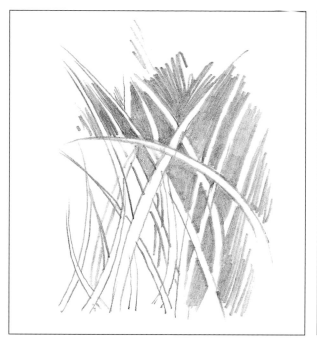

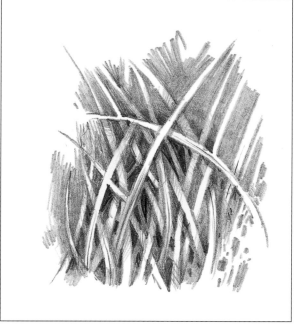

Delineating Contrasts If we lightly draw guidelines for some blades of overlapping grass, and then shade the middle values in the negative spaces, we define those grasses. This composition repeats the actively opposing elements of the grasses, contrasting them with the rectangular negative spaces.

Developing Complexity and Unity Intricacy is developed in the composition by working darker values into the negative spaces, as well as by shading the grasses. The composition becomes more interesting through the negative space, which unifies the grass into one mass.

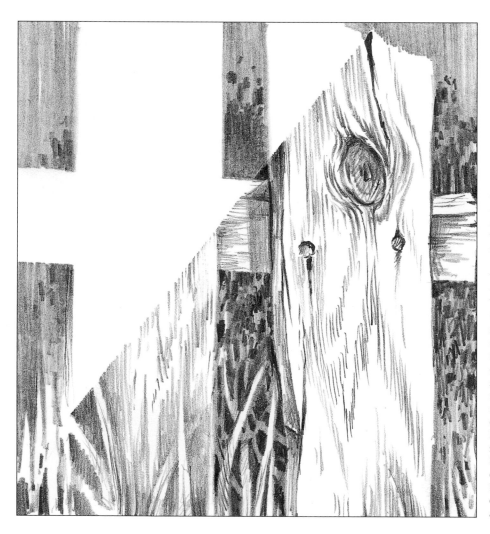

◄ **Creating Depth and Repetition** At the upper left of this sketch, the shape of the old wooden fence is created by drawing objects in the negative spaces around it; dark and light value patterns suggest distant sky and foliage. As the drawing progresses to the right, the white boards are shaded to create texture and shadows. Within the positive space, the knot, nails, grain, and even splits in the wood are repetitions of shapes and values seen in the negative spaces and foreground grasses. Within the negative space, patterns of secondary negative shapes develop as more darks are added to convey depth (such as the space between blades of grass.) The single horizontal board and sky help contrast the mainly vertical elements while offering clear indications of depth. The overall composition is simple, familiar, and comfortable for the viewer.

COMPOSING FROM PHOTOGRAPHS

Photos are great references for creating compositions. Use one photo or take elements from a number of photos and combine them in one composition. Create several different compositions from one photo; just crop the photo in a way that emphasizes the main elements and makes a statement about them. If there is an interesting element outside the selected area, it can be moved to a comfortable position within the scene. Unneeded elements can be eliminated. Use "artistic license" (the artist's prerogative to ignore or change reality) to add detail. When composing a scene from photos, look for the qualities that make a dynamic composition: depth through shadows and overlapping, asymmetrical placement, rhythm and flow, value contrasts, interesting lines and textures, and balance.

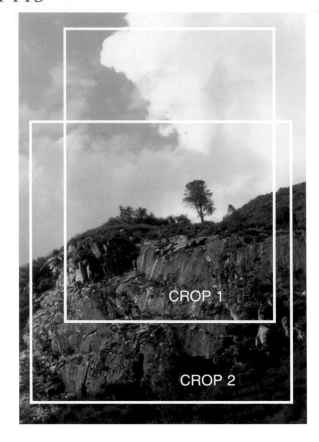

▶ **Shifting Focal Points** In crop 1 at right, much of the vertical cliff face is cut away; the lone tree is the central focal point, and the clouds and cliff rocks are balanced secondary elements. In crop 2, the cliff face becomes a much stronger element, drawing the eye first, then leading up to the tree.

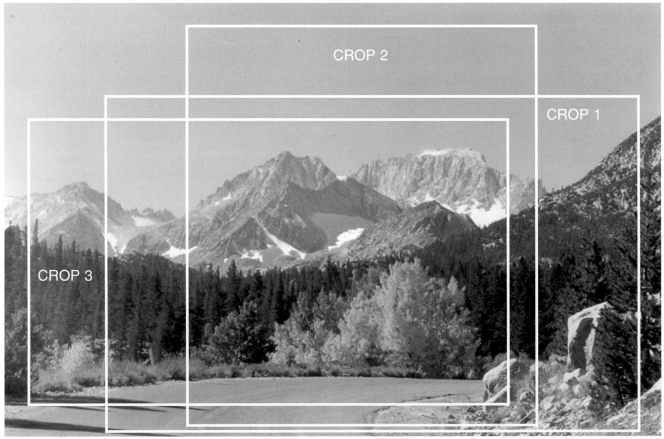

Three Crops from One Photo The trees, mountains, and sky shown here provide the source for three different compositions. Each crop accents an important part of the scene. Lay strips of paper around each crop to isolate it and study the differences.

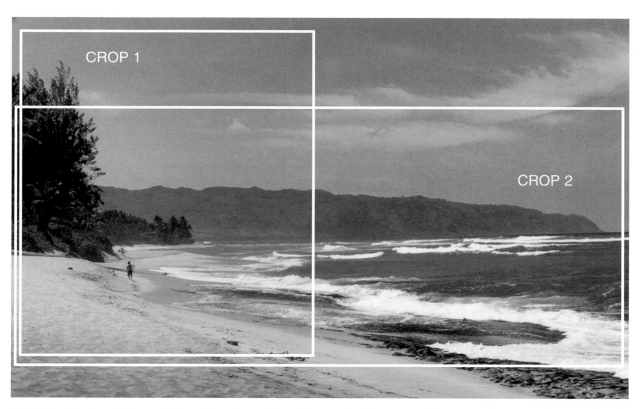

CROP 1

CROP 2

Vertical and Horizontal Crops This beautiful beach scene in Hawaii is an example of how two very different compositions can come from one photo. The vertical crop (1) accents the lone person with the open sky and foreground beach. The horizontal crop (2)—my favorite—accents the long expanse of land and sea and makes the individual on the beach appear much smaller and isolated.

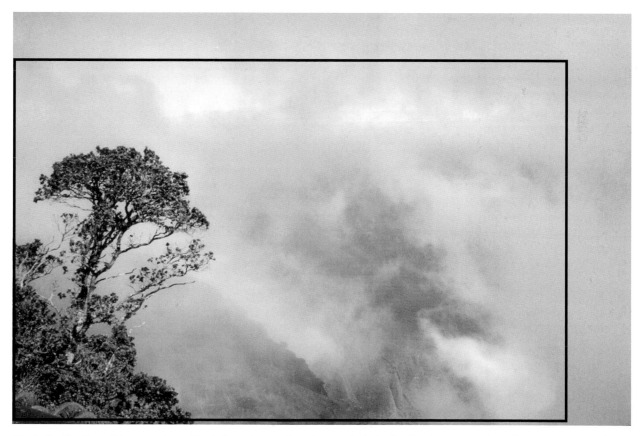

Maximize the Crop This photo, taken on Kauai, shows the mysterious afternoon clouds that float into the canyons. The single crop removes featureless cloud areas and focuses the viewer's eye on the foreground tree against the dramatic cloud formation.

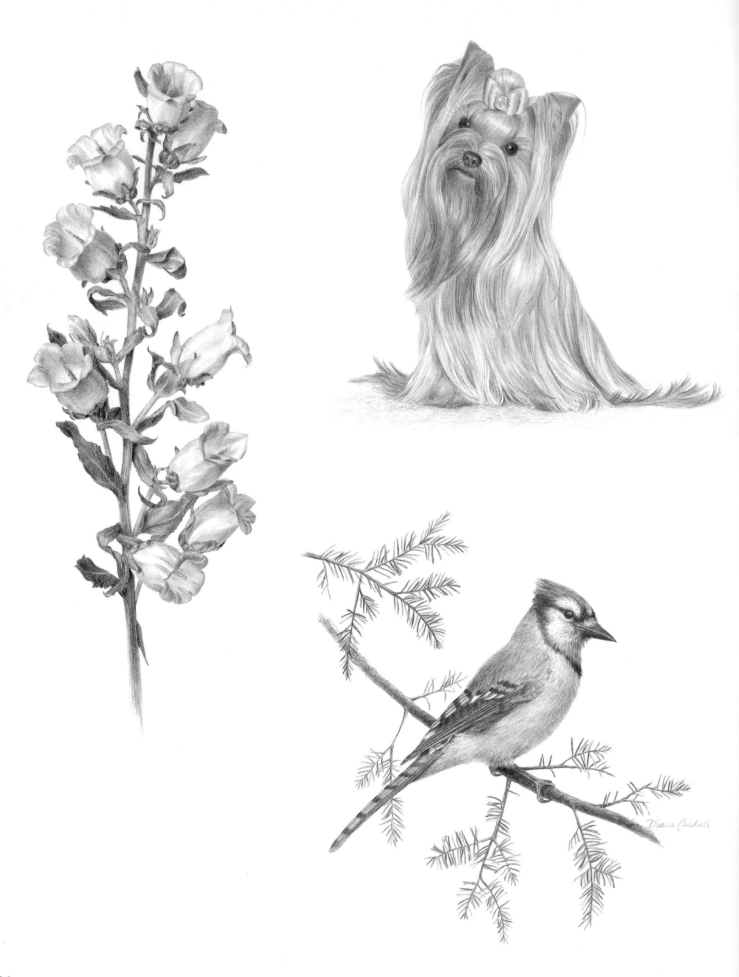

84

CHAPTER 3
REALISTIC TEXTURES

with Diane Cardaci

Over the years, my continuous fascination with texture has inspired me to use the pencil as a powerful tool of artistic expression. I have learned from teachers and fellow artists, as well as from studying the drawings of the Old Masters. Some of my favorite techniques, however, have come from just taking the time to experiment with hand position, pressure, the grade of the graphite, and different types of papers. This chapter is designed to share some tried-and-true techniques, as well as to inspire you to play with pencil textures. In addition to standard step-by-step lessons, I've also included creative exercises that focus on your artistic nature. Explore the world of textures and see what you can create on your own. See what your pencil is truly capable of and let it become a part of your creative palette. Enjoy!

—*Diane Cardaci*

About Diane Cardaci

Having drawn and painted since she was a child, Diane Cardaci was classically trained at the Art Students League of New York City, Parsons School of Design, and the School of Visual Arts. Her passion for both realism and nature led her to start her professional art career working as a Natural Science Illustrator in New York City. Her work has been published by the American Museum of Natural History in New York City, as well as by major textbook companies. Diane was also the director of her own art school, the Academy of Classical Art in West Palm Beach, Florida, for four years. She is a Signature member of the American Society of Portrait Artists and has contributed writing for the organization's publications. Diane is also a member of the Colored Pencil Society of America, the Graphic Artists Guild, and the Illustrator's Partnership of America.

"PAINTING" WITH PENCIL

When you use painterly strokes, your drawing will take on a new dimension. Think of your pencil as a brush and allow yourself to put more of your arm into the stroke. To create this effect, I usually hold my pencil between my thumb and forefinger and use the side of the pencil. (See page 6.) If you rotate the pencil in your hand every few strokes, you will not have to sharpen it as frequently. The larger the lead, the wider the stroke will be. The softer the lead, the more painterly an effect you will have. These examples were all made on smooth paper with a 6B pencil, but you can experiment with rough papers for more broken effects.

Starting Simply First I experiment with vertical, horizontal, and curved strokes. I keep the strokes close together and begin with heavy pressure. Then I lighten the pressure with each stroke.

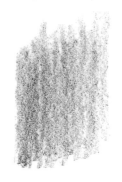
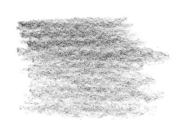

Varying the Pressure Here I randomly cover the area with tone, varying the pressure at different points. I continue to keep my strokes loose.

Using Smaller Strokes I make small circles for the first example. This reminds me of leathery animal skin. For the second example (at far right), I use short, alternating strokes of heavy and light pressure, similar to a stone or brick pattern.

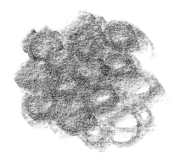
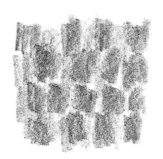

Loosening Up At right, I use vertical strokes. Varying the pressure for each stroke, I start to see long grass. At the far right, I use somewhat looser movements that could be used for water. First I create short spiral movements with my arm (above). Then I use a wavy movement, varying the pressure (below).

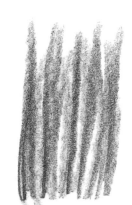

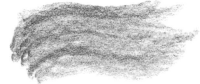

WORKING WITH DIFFERENT TECHNIQUES

Below are several examples of techniques that can be done with pencil. These techniques are important for creating more painterly effects in your drawing. Remember that B pencils have soft lead and H pencils have hard lead—you will need to use both for these exercises.

Creating Washes Create a watercolor effect by blending water-soluble pencil shading with a wet brush. Make sure your brush isn't too wet, and use thicker paper, such as vellum board.

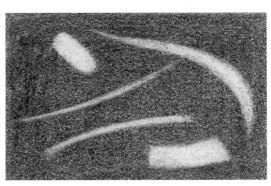

Lifting Out Blend a soft pencil on smooth paper, and then lift out the desired area of graphite with an eraser. You can create highlights and other interesting effects with this technique.

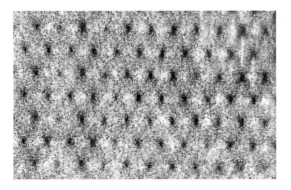

Rubbing Place paper over an object and rub the side of your pencil lead over the paper. The strokes of your pencil will pick up the pattern and replicate it on the paper. Try using a soft pencil on smooth paper, and choose an object with a strong textural pattern. For this example, I used a wire grid.

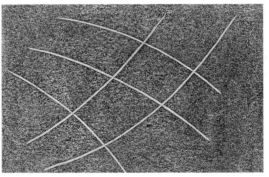

Producing Indented Lines Draw a pattern or design on the paper with a sharp, non-marking object, like a knitting needle or skewer, before drawing with a pencil. When you shade over the area with the side of your pencil, the graphite will not reach the indented areas, leaving white lines.

Smudging

Smudging is an important technique for creating shading and gradients. Use a tortillon, blending stump, or chamois cloth to blend your strokes. It is important to not use your finger, because your hand, even if clean, has natural oils that can damage your art.

Smudging on Rough Surfaces Use a 6B pencil on vellum-finish Bristol board. Make your strokes with the side of the pencil and blend. In this example, the effect is very granular.

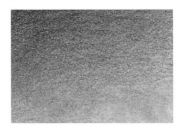

Smudging on Smooth Surfaces Use a 4B pencil on plate-finish Bristol board. Stroke with the side of the pencil, and then blend your strokes with a blending stump.

Combining Techniques

Various techniques can be combined to create very unique effects. By experimenting with them, you can see how many different effects you can create by just changing your pencil, the amount of pressure you place on the pencil, or your hand position. For example, making an indented line and applying tone over it is a great way to show the fine veins of a leaf. By letting loose, you may come across an accidental technique that is perfect for what you are trying to express.

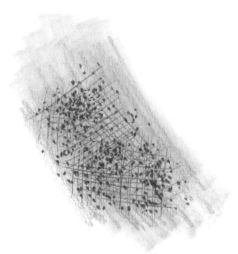

Crosshatching and Stippling I use the side of a 2B pencil, and quickly stroke back and forth across the paper in a zigzag manner. Next I take a sharp HB and create cross-hatched lines on top. I switch to a large lead holder with a 6B lead and use heavy pressure to put some stipple on top. This effect reminds me of a chain link fence covered by flowers.

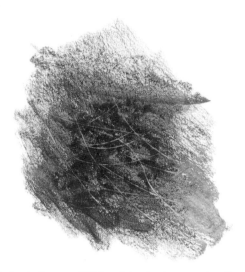

Indentations and Water Before I make any marks with the pencil, I use a knitting needle to make impressions in the paper. Then I use the side of a water-soluble pencil to lay down some tone. Next I take a wet watercolor brush and smear the graphite. This technique is very useful when you want to create a scratchy, rough look, such as old leather or weathered metal.

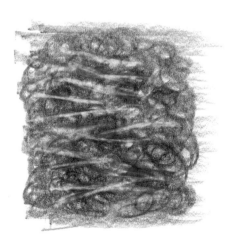

Smearing and Lifting Smudging is a great technique for rendering softer textures, such as fur. I use a soft 6B pencil to make some horizontal strokes and then lightly smear them with a blending stump. On top of this, I place some very heavy, curved, short strokes. Then I use my kneaded eraser to lift out random spots of graphite. This texture is reminiscent of a nubby sweater.

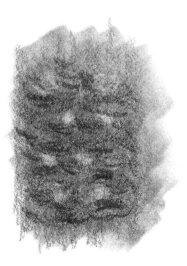

Using Textured Paper and Soft Pencil Here you can see how rough paper combined with a soft pencil creates the appearance of rocky dirt. I use a vellum paper and draw with the side of a 6B. I put down heavy tone and dab a few spots with my kneaded eraser, but I don't have to worry much about texture because the paper is creating it for me. Then I use a sharp 2B to draw a few individual rocks. I evoke the feeling of a gravelly road without adding much detail.

FOLLOWING FORM

In addition to creating form, light also creates the texture of an object. As the light falls across an object with a strong texture, each individual aspect of the texture will create its own light and shadow effect. But these individual value changes must remain secondary to the form shadows, or the form will be lost. For example, if you draw a very thick texture all over an object and forget to include highlights to show the object's shape, the object will appear to be flat and without depth.

When you are drawing an object with texture, first imagine it as a smooth object with no texture at all. I like to think of the texture of the object as a sort of translucent coat, so the underlying values of the form will show through. It is good practice to draw a few textured objects and develop a light, middle, and dark value for each of the objects. Then look at how the form changes as the values change.

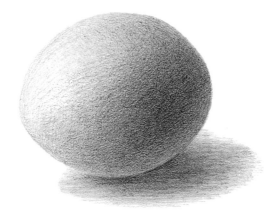

Seeing Form A coconut (shown above as being lit from a three-quarter angle) has a form similar to that of an egg. I imagine the coconut with a smooth, egglike surface. Once I understand the way the light is hitting the object, I can draw its form.

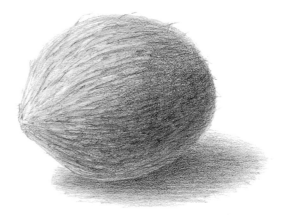

Form vs. Texture A coconut is a good example of texture versus form. You might be tempted to use dark, heavy shading to portray the coconut's surface. However, in this case, the coconut's form is more important than its texture.

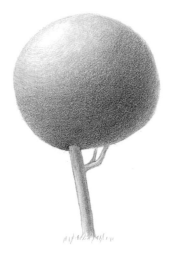

Studying Shapes To understand how the light source creates the form of this tree, I break down the tree into a ball and a cylinder. I use rough paper to add some texture, and I put down a layer of dark tone with the side of the pencil.

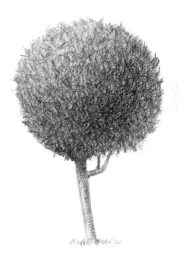

Adding Detail Using short strokes, I create the leaves. Don't get caught up in drawing individual leaves—instead suggest the leaves with a pattern of texture. As I draw the leaves, I leave the texture lighter on top where the light source hits the tree.

BOTANICAL TEXTURES

Botanical drawings are portraits of plants that are drawn with realism. They show the beauty of flowers and other plants with their intricate and delicate detail.

Flowers make great subjects because the bright colors challenge you to create tones that evoke their vivid nature. However, botanical compositions contain more than just flowers. Trees and other flowerless plants make wonderful subjects as well.

When drawing plants, it is important to remember that leaves come in many shapes, sizes, and textures. Besides their general shape, their edges (irregular or smooth), shininess (glossy or matte), and thickness must be carefully observed. It can be quite interesting to capture the unique qualities of each plant. So don't just stop and smell the roses—pull out your pencil and sketch them!

Parts of a Flower

stigma

pistil

petal

anther

stamen

style

sepal

ovary

filament

stem

Flower Detail A flower is made up of more than just petals and leaves. There are many small details that you should be familiar with to be able to bring realism to your art. This diagram shows the different parts of a flower that will be referred to in some of the step-by-step lessons; this diagram also will help you in your future sketches.

Leaves

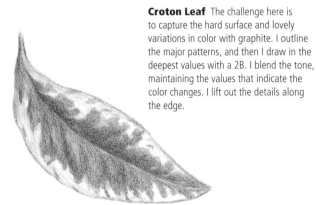

Croton Leaf The challenge here is to capture the hard surface and lovely variations in color with graphite. I outline the major patterns, and then I draw in the deepest values with a 2B. I blend the tone, maintaining the values that indicate the color changes. I lift out the details along the edge.

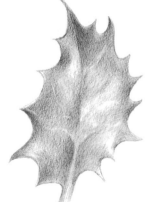

Holly Leaf With the side of a 2B, I lay in some tone. I smudge the tone and lift out any areas that should remain white. The highlights will be important for creating the appearance of this leaf's glossy shine. I add deeper tones with a 4B (accenting the sharp points of the leaves and the raised veins), and then I blend. I lift out the lighter veins.

Petals

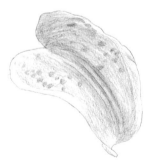

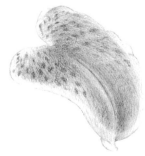

Step 1 I draw the outline of the petal, then add the general shape of the coloration, some of the darker spots, and the raised center area. The strokes emphasize the petal's softness. Next I darken the irregular spots and deepen the area along the center of the petal to bring out the raised parts.

Step 2 I deepen the shading of the colored areas, using long strokes that follow the direction of the petal and bring out its smoothness. I darken the markings and the center line, and then I lightly shade the area where the petal folds back on itself.

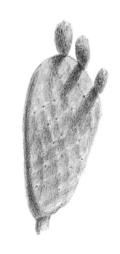

Cactus Leaf The dark shading along the edge of this leaf defines its thickness. I add the shadows cast by the cactus fruit. I shade the diamond-shaped depressions on the leaf with a 2B, and I lift out the raised areas. I place dots to emphasize the points where the sharp spines connect to the cactus.

BELLFLOWER

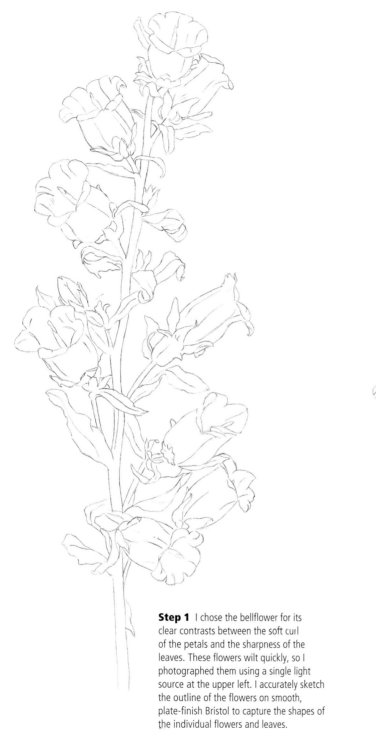

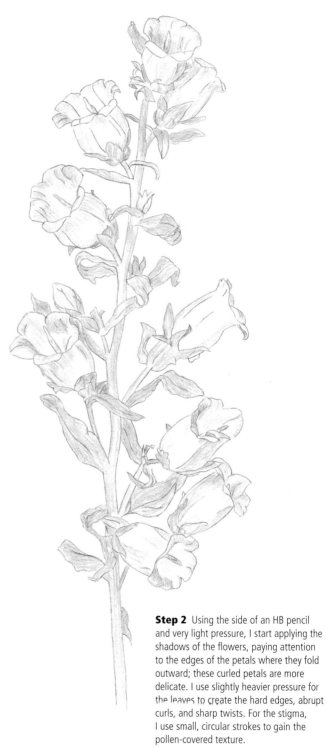

Step 1 I chose the bellflower for its clear contrasts between the soft curl of the petals and the sharpness of the leaves. These flowers wilt quickly, so I photographed them using a single light source at the upper left. I accurately sketch the outline of the flowers on smooth, plate-finish Bristol to capture the shapes of the individual flowers and leaves.

Step 2 Using the side of an HB pencil and very light pressure, I start applying the shadows of the flowers, paying attention to the edges of the petals where they fold outward; these curled petals are more delicate. I use slightly heavier pressure for the leaves to create the hard edges, abrupt curls, and sharp twists. For the stigma, I use small, circular strokes to gain the pollen-covered texture.

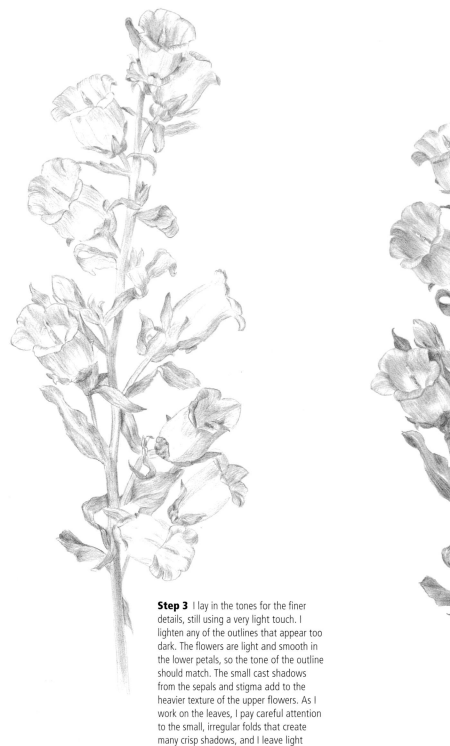

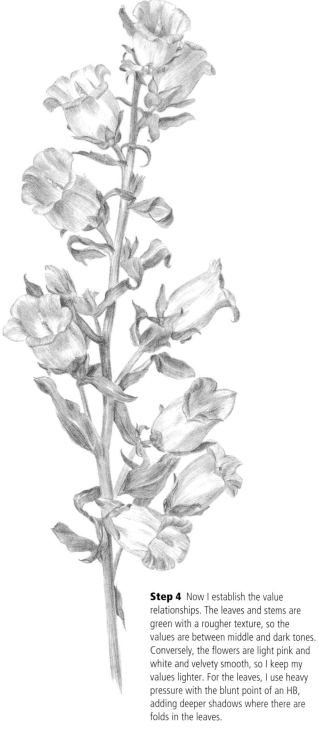

Step 3 I lay in the tones for the finer details, still using a very light touch. I lighten any of the outlines that appear too dark. The flowers are light and smooth in the lower petals, so the tone of the outline should match. The small cast shadows from the sepals and stigma add to the heavier texture of the upper flowers. As I work on the leaves, I pay careful attention to the small, irregular folds that create many crisp shadows, and I leave light areas for the leaf veins.

Step 4 Now I establish the value relationships. The leaves and stems are green with a rougher texture, so the values are between middle and dark tones. Conversely, the flowers are light pink and white and velvety smooth, so I keep my values lighter. For the leaves, I use heavy pressure with the blunt point of an HB, adding deeper shadows where there are folds in the leaves.

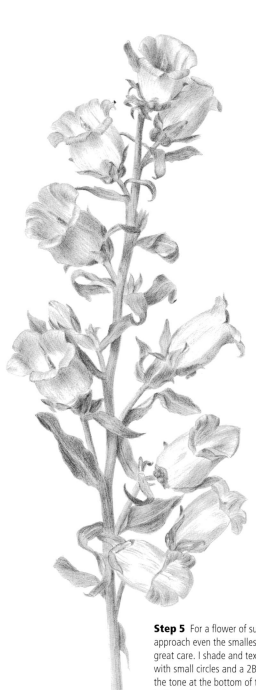

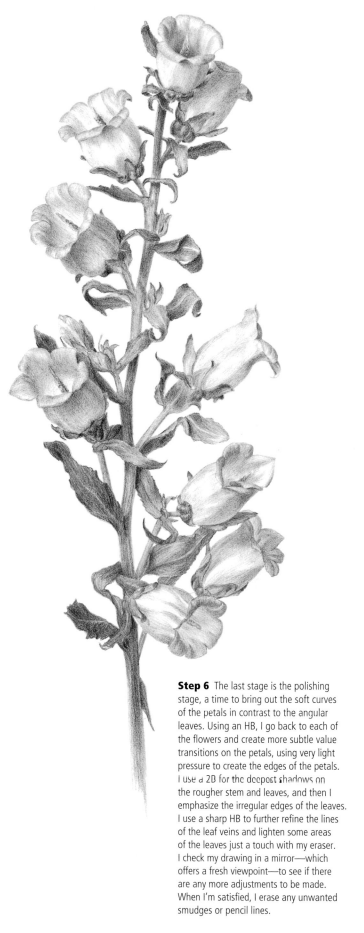

Step 5 For a flower of such delicacy, I approach even the smallest details with great care. I shade and texture the stigma with small circles and a 2B and deepen the tone at the bottom of the stigma to indicate the cast shadow. I add a little stippling on top for more texture. Using an HB, I go over each flower, deepening the shading to bring out the cup shape. I then use my kneaded eraser to lift out the lightest parts of the flowers, particularly where the petals fold out. Where the leaves fold over and create shadows, I use heavy pressure to create dark tones. I further deepen the shading on the stem; then I lift out highlights and some leaf veins with my kneaded eraser.

Step 6 The last stage is the polishing stage, a time to bring out the soft curves of the petals in contrast to the angular leaves. Using an HB, I go back to each of the flowers and create more subtle value transitions on the petals, using very light pressure to create the edges of the petals. I use a 2B for the deepest shadows on the rougher stem and leaves, and then I emphasize the irregular edges of the leaves. I use a sharp HB to further refine the lines of the leaf veins and lighten some areas of the leaves just a touch with my eraser. I check my drawing in a mirror—which offers a fresh viewpoint—to see if there are any more adjustments to be made. When I'm satisfied, I erase any unwanted smudges or pencil lines.

TRADITIONAL STILL LIFE TEXTURES

Still life compositions allow you to have complete control: You design the composition; choose the range of textures, values, and colors; and create the ideal lighting situation. I like to set up my compositions so that there are many contrasting textures, such as a smooth piece of fruit in a coarsely woven basket. Play around with different types of fruits and cheeses to see how the light catches their textures. It's always an added bonus to be able to share your food subject after your drawing is done!

Fruit

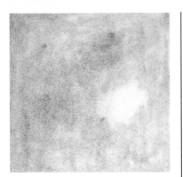

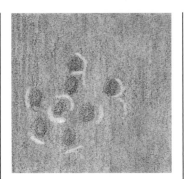
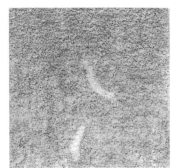

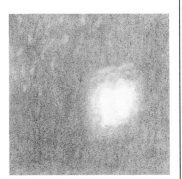
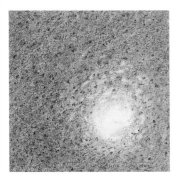
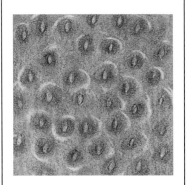
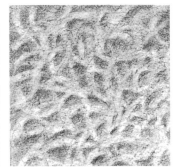

Apple A polished red apple reflects a strong highlight, which contrasts with the skin's dark tone. I apply carbon dust (shavings I collected from sharpening my pencils) with circular, irregular strokes (top), then lift out the highlight with an eraser (bottom).

Orange First I apply carbon dust, using strokes that follow the fruit's form (top). I lift out the main highlight and then use an eraser to create curved strokes around the highlight, showing the bumpy texture of the orange's skin (bottom).

Strawberry I lay in dark tone with carbon dust and use a 4B to start establishing a dotted pattern for the strawberry (top). I continue to enhance the dimpled, seeded texture by adding thin, curved highlight lines around the darker dots (bottom).

Cantaloupe With the side of a 4B, I lay down some tone and then randomly blend the graphite. I lift out a few lines to see how the lights contrast with the dark tone (top). Because the skin is very rough, there are no highlights—just the upper veining.

Baskets

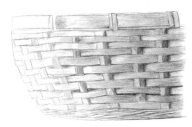

Weaves Baskets are incredibly tactile. The texture of the weave creates a three-dimensional pattern with many layers. Trying your hand at rendering a woven basket is a great way to learn about the interplay of light and shadow and how it can show the heavy texture of the basket.

Wood

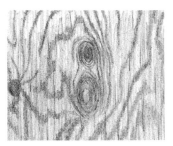
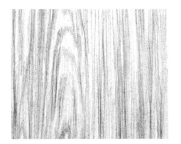
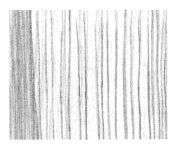

Knotty Pine Zigzagged lines create the rough pattern of the grain. I use concentric ovals to draw the knots. Then I use an HB to add light, straight vertical strokes and individual shorter strokes to show the raised grain.

Ash For this fine-grained wood, I make long, inverted U shapes with a slightly uneven motion. Then I draw very long grain lines, varying their density and allowing the lines to curve naturally. I go over these lines with light, vertical lines.

Zebrawood With a 4B, I create the dark lines of this straight-grained hardwood. I group some closer together to indicate the color variation. I use a 2H to add very light tone with long, vertical strokes, adding a smooth quality.

WINE AND CHEESE

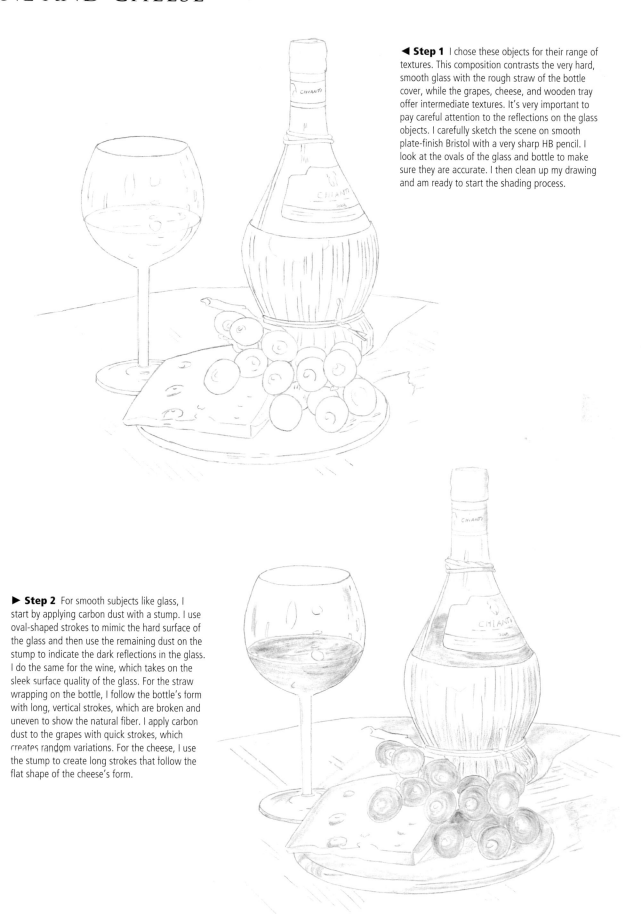

◄ **Step 1** I chose these objects for their range of textures. This composition contrasts the very hard, smooth glass with the rough straw of the bottle cover, while the grapes, cheese, and wooden tray offer intermediate textures. It's very important to pay careful attention to the reflections on the glass objects. I carefully sketch the scene on smooth plate-finish Bristol with a very sharp HB pencil. I look at the ovals of the glass and bottle to make sure they are accurate. I then clean up my drawing and am ready to start the shading process.

► **Step 2** For smooth subjects like glass, I start by applying carbon dust with a stump. I use oval-shaped strokes to mimic the hard surface of the glass and then use the remaining dust on the stump to indicate the dark reflections in the glass. I do the same for the wine, which takes on the sleek surface quality of the glass. For the straw wrapping on the bottle, I follow the bottle's form with long, vertical strokes, which are broken and uneven to show the natural fiber. I apply carbon dust to the grapes with quick strokes, which creates random variations. For the cheese, I use the stump to create long strokes that follow the flat shape of the cheese's form.

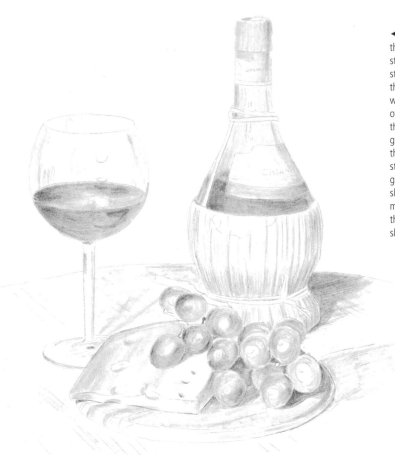

◄ **Step 3** Building up the glassy surface of the wine, I use a 2B pencil to create long, curved strokes; then I blend with my stump. I use vertical strokes for the rigid stem of the glass where there are reflections, and I use curved strokes where there are some darker tones at the base of the glass. I add light shading on the labels of the bottle. For the straw, I blend the first layer of graphite and use the side of the 2B to establish the soft shadows created by the overlapping straw. I add some dark form shadows to the grapes and then blend my strokes to create the slick skin. I add more tone to the cheese with my stump, and then I darken the depression in the cheese with my pencil. I add tone to the cast shadows on the table and then blend the strokes.

► **Step 4** Following the contours of the forms, I use a 2H pencil to add some shading to the glass, stem, and base to give them sharp, crisp edges. Returning to the bottle, I darken the wine using my 2B. At the back of the bottle where the reflections are, I blend even further, adding to the smoothness of the surface. I also add to the reflections in the glass by using the stump. I deepen the grapes and use a sharp HB to redefine the grapes' distinct edges. I use the side of the pencil for the thin stems of the grapes. For the creamy cheese, I shade using light strokes with my HB, following the direction of the form, and then I darken the wax rind with a 4B. I refine the delicate wood grain with an HB and draw in some details on the bottle labels.

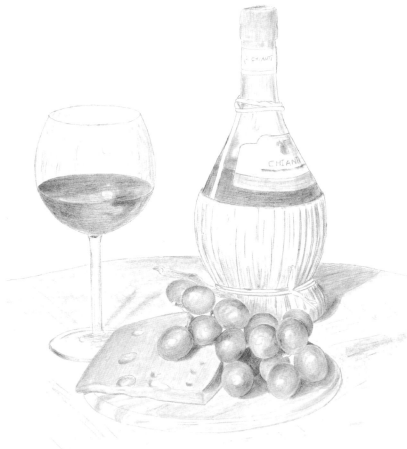

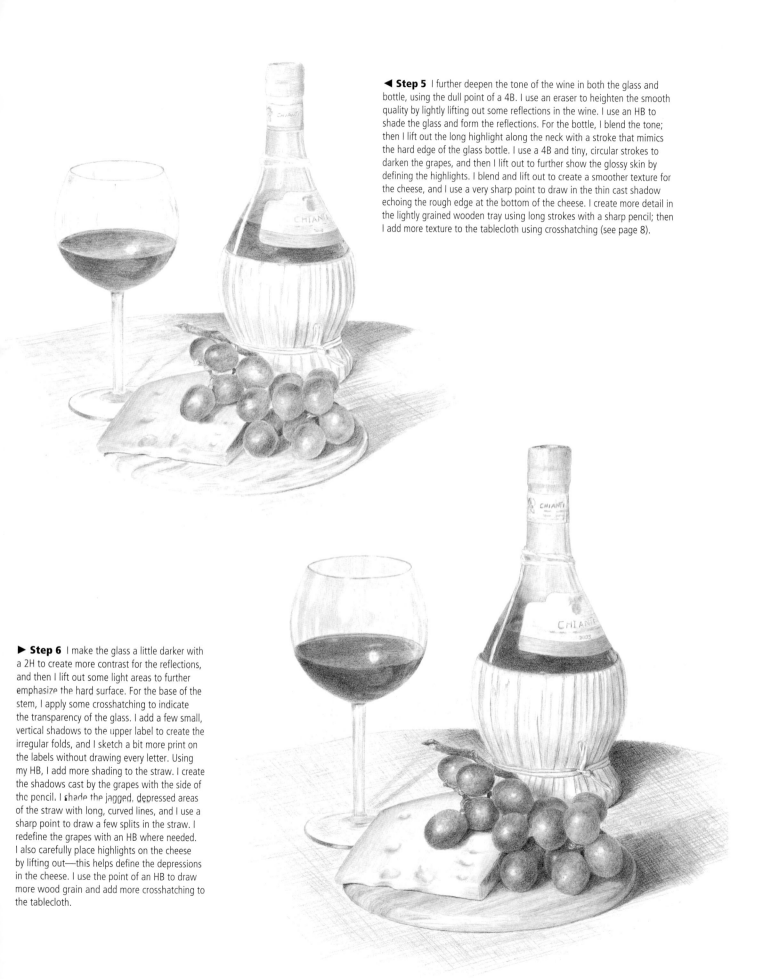

◄ Step 5 I further deepen the tone of the wine in both the glass and bottle, using the dull point of a 4B. I use an eraser to heighten the smooth quality by lightly lifting out some reflections in the wine. I use an HB to shade the glass and form the reflections. For the bottle, I blend the tone; then I lift out the long highlight along the neck with a stroke that mimics the hard edge of the glass bottle. I use a 4B and tiny, circular strokes to darken the grapes, and then I lift out to further show the glossy skin by defining the highlights. I blend and lift out to create a smoother texture for the cheese, and I use a very sharp point to draw in the thin cast shadow echoing the rough edge at the bottom of the cheese. I create more detail in the lightly grained wooden tray using long strokes with a sharp pencil; then I add more texture to the tablecloth using crosshatching (see page 8).

► Step 6 I make the glass a little darker with a 2H to create more contrast for the reflections, and then I lift out some light areas to further emphasize the hard surface. For the base of the stem, I apply some crosshatching to indicate the transparency of the glass. I add a few small, vertical shadows to the upper label to create the irregular folds, and I sketch a bit more print on the labels without drawing every letter. Using my HB, I add more shading to the straw. I create the shadows cast by the grapes with the side of the pencil. I shade the jagged, depressed areas of the straw with long, curved lines, and I use a sharp point to draw a few splits in the straw. I redefine the grapes with an HB where needed. I also carefully place highlights on the cheese by lifting out—this helps define the depressions in the cheese. I use the point of an HB to draw more wood grain and add more crosshatching to the tablecloth.

FLORAL STILL LIFE TEXTURES

Flowers come in so many interesting forms, colors, and textures—it's no wonder they are an endless inspiration for artists! When setting up a floral still life, keep your containers and arrangements simple, with a textural quality that won't overwhelm the flowers.

Glass

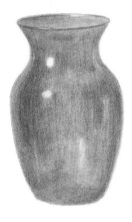

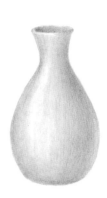

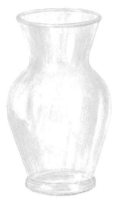

Opaque Gloss Vase I apply carbon dust, and then I lift out the bright highlights. For the subtle highlights, I drag my eraser lightly across the tone of the vase.

Opaque Matte Vase This vase hardly has any highlights. I use an HB and make crisp edges to show the hard, smooth surface.

Clear Vase This vase is transparent, so the back of the vase can be seen from the front. There also are sharp highlights and reflections. I use a 2H for shading.

Ceramic

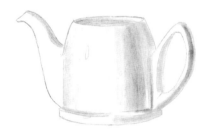

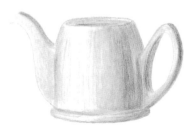

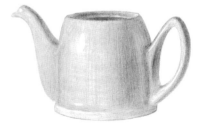

Step 1 Glazed ceramic clay is very hard and reflective. I create a "wash" with carbon dust and a stump, then establish the shadow patterns. My vertical strokes follow the form of the teapot.

Step 2 I go back with a sharp HB and draw light, vertical strokes that follow the contour of the teapot. Then I use strokes that reach across the teapot horizontally, particularly around the base.

Step 3 I build up the values of the teapot with vertical and horizontal strokes, and then I use the stump to blend. For crisp contrasts, I use an eraser to lift out highlights and spots of reflected light.

Fabrics

▶ **Fringe** I use a sharp HB to draw a detailed outline of the fringe and knots. The strands should be slightly frayed, reflecting the softness of the thread.

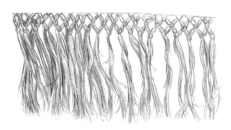

▶ **Crochet** Lace and crocheted fabrics have holes that add a lovely textural element. The holes create heavy shadow, but the fabric is still light and delicate.

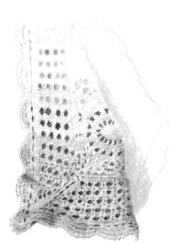

PITCHER OF LILIES

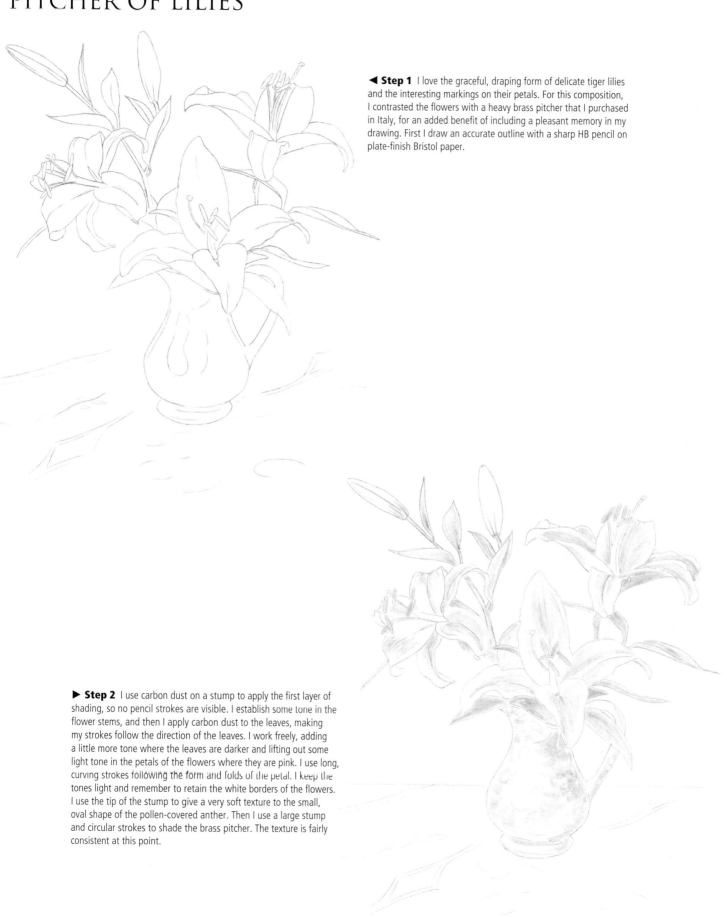

◄ **Step 1** I love the graceful, draping form of delicate tiger lilies and the interesting markings on their petals. For this composition, I contrasted the flowers with a heavy brass pitcher that I purchased in Italy, for an added benefit of including a pleasant memory in my drawing. First I draw an accurate outline with a sharp HB pencil on plate-finish Bristol paper.

► **Step 2** I use carbon dust on a stump to apply the first layer of shading, so no pencil strokes are visible. I establish some tone in the flower stems, and then I apply carbon dust to the leaves, making my strokes follow the direction of the leaves. I work freely, adding a little more tone where the leaves are darker and lifting out some light tone in the petals of the flowers where they are pink. I use long, curving strokes following the form and folds of the petal. I keep the tones light and remember to retain the white borders of the flowers. I use the tip of the stump to give a very soft texture to the small, oval shape of the pollen-covered anther. Then I use a large stump and circular strokes to shade the brass pitcher. The texture is fairly consistent at this point.

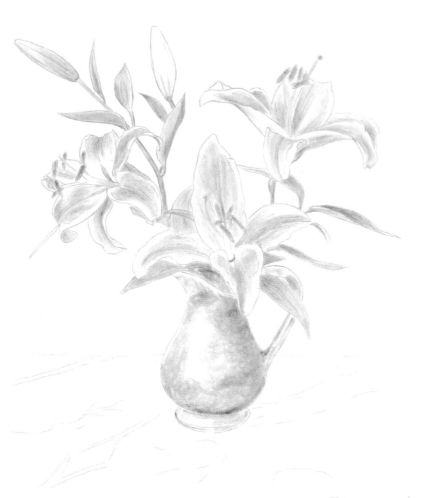

◄ Step 3 I use a 2B pencil to add more tone to the stems, using long strokes along the length of the stems to show their strength and smooth lines. I do the same with the leaves. Then I carefully start adding tone to the petals. The color value is usually darker in the center and at the base of the petal, so I use a little more pressure in these places. I use a 6B to add a bit more texture to the anthers and the stigma. I shade the style with a 2B and use a curved, dark stroke at the base of the flower where the pistil and stamen emerge. There are two buds that have not yet opened, so I add just a little shading where their soft petals join the stem. I deepen the values of the pitcher using circular strokes, and then I blend the strokes. I place darker tone at the base of the pitcher and along the handle.

► Step 4 I return to the stems and leaves to fully establish their even textures and the value of their green color, which is much darker than the value of the pink petals. I use a 2B, again using long strokes, to deepen the shadowed side of the stem by going over it with the point of a small stump. I shade the leaves, and I use a 4B in the darkest areas, such as at the base of the arrangement. While I am working on the leaves, I begin to alternate between a pencil and a blending stump. I allow some strokes to be more obvious to capture the appearance of the veining in the leaves. I also darken the undersides of some of the petals, keeping the strokes very soft looking. I take my 6B pencil and use the side of it to shade the pitcher irregularly. Then I lift out to maintain the highlight. I add some tone to the table where the cast shadow falls and then wipe it with a chamois cloth to smooth it.

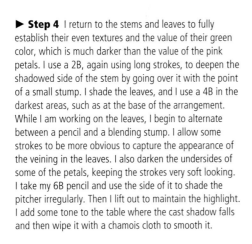

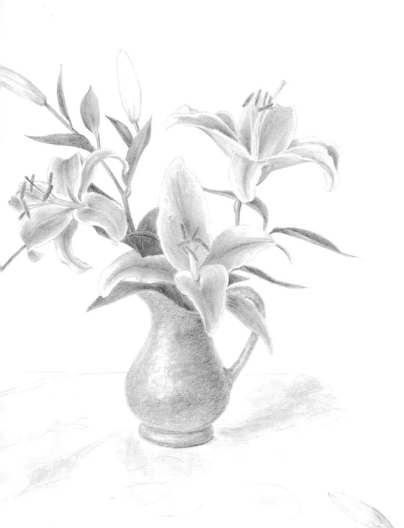

◄ **Step 5** At this point, my values and forms are well established, so I focus on refining the shading to show more texture. I use a pencil, a stump, and an eraser to create even tones and delicate transitions between strokes. I use the point of my pencil for small cast and form shadows, such as where the buds and the base of the leaf attach to the stem. I delicately shade the tight, smooth buds using an HB and long, light strokes. I smooth the tone on the velvety, soft petals and then touch up the edges, further defining the petals. I use a 4B with tiny, circular strokes to shade the anthers, adding to their pollen-laden roughness. I add more tone to the pitcher with a 6B, keeping it darkest on the side that is farthest away from the light and leaving the strokes rough to show the metallic texture. I lightly lift some tone from the edge of the right side of the pitcher to indicate the reflected light.

▶ **Step 6** I again darken the leaves with smooth, steady strokes, and then I use my kneaded eraser to lift out some thin venation lines. For the petals, I further refine the tonal shading using an HB, a stump, and an eraser. I lift out the white borders of the petals, and I add the flat spots that are so characteristic of the lilies. I also define the stamens and the pistils, strengthening the tone at the base of the flower where they merge. I smooth out the tones of the pitcher using a 4B with small, circular strokes, and then use the point of the pencil to better define the edges of the hard metal where there is a thin line of shadow at the base. I stipple in some dots with a 6B and randomly dab with the tip of the eraser to create the feel of the pitting. I add very light tone on the table using horizontal strokes with the side of the pencil. I use just a little pressure to deepen the embroidery pattern of the tablecloth. I also darken the shadow cast by the arrangement.

101

WILDLIFE TEXTURES

Nature provides some of the most exquisite and interesting textures. Drawing wildlife is especially helpful because each animal comprises a number of different textural elements. Think about a bird with its sleek feathers, scaly feet, smooth beak, and glistening eyes. What more could an artist ask for?

In my backyard, there is a wealth of textures just waiting to challenge me, from a delicate butterfly to a scruffy groundhog. All of the textures on this page can be found right outside my door. What is waiting outside your door?

Feathers

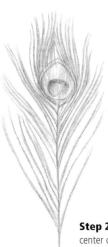

Step 1 To capture the wispy, fragile texture of a peacock's feather, I start by drawing thin lines that stem from a vertical centerline. Then I draw a circle within an oval for the "eye"— I draw the curved lines that surround the "eye" so that they follow the ovular form.

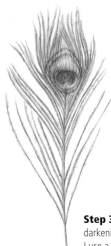

Step 2 I darken the center of the "eye" to emphasize the peacock feather's distinctive pattern. I keep the area around the center very light to indicate the change in color and the delicate feather texture.

Step 3 After darkening all my lines, I use a kneaded eraser to lift out a small curve along the edge of the dark center. (See "Lifting Out for Feathers" at right for more information.)

Lifting Out for Feathers

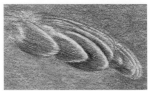

Here I use an eraser to lift out the white edges of the feathers. I go back in and reinforce the edges with pencil to show the defined edges of the feathers. It often is difficult to control the shape of the edges of the lifted area, so the delicacy of the edges can be lost. I use short lines that follow the direction of the feathers to create additional texture. Then I blend the background with an eraser to help make the feathers stand out.

Scales and Skin

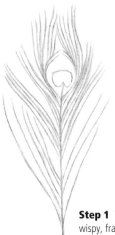

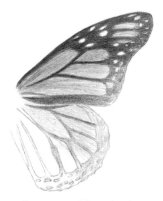

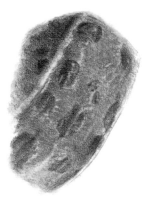

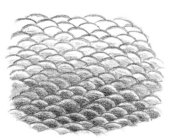

Alligator I use a soft, broad pencil with plate-finish paper, as I don't want the effects of rough paper to interfere with the leathery, bumpy texture of the alligator's skin. Pay attention to the direction of the light source when dealing with textures— alligator skin is made up of many small ridges, and each ridge must be lit properly for the drawing to appear realistic.

Butterfly First I carefully outline the drawing with a sharp HB pencil. I lightly draw the very thin veins, using long strokes. I go back in and put down another layer of tone, this time also covering the lighter areas of the wing. Next I use a 2B pencil to deepen the veins, gradually increasing the pressure on my pencil and using long strokes that follow the shape of the wing. I switch back to the HB and use long strokes to deepen the light tones of the wing, allowing some strokes to be darker to create a slight variation in the soft tones within the lighter area.

Frog Frog skin is usually moist, so using the smudging technique (see page 87) seemed appropriate. I use darker tones to create the raised bumps and lift out some graphite to add highlights to the slimy surface to give a wet look to the entire skin.

Fish First I outline the scales, paying careful attention to the details. Then I add shading at the base of the scales where they overlap to show the distinctive flaky texture. Note that every scale has been given a highlight—this helps capture the fish's shimmery nature.

BLUE JAY

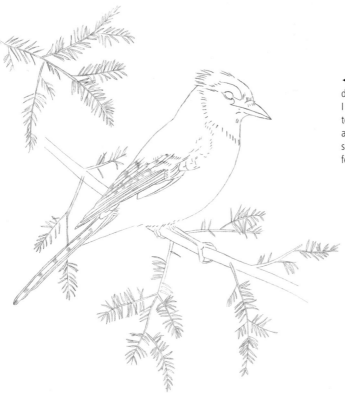

◄ Step 1 I begin this drawing with a carefully detailed outline drawn with a sharp HB mechanical pencil. When drawing the head, I use short strokes to create the softer edges of the feathers. I refer to several photos to confirm that the feather patterns are accurate, and I indicate the black markings of the bird with some quick shading. Right now I am more concerned with capturing the basic features of the bird—details will come later.

► Step 2 With a sharp 2H pencil, I darken the lines around the feathers to define them, and I add some dark markings using short strokes. At this stage I am still very concerned about the accuracy of the feather patterns, as markings on the wings and tail are very important in identifying a bird. As I draw, I make sure that all of my strokes follow the direction of the feathers—even at this early stage, texture is being created by my strokes. I shade under the wings, but I don't want the shadows to be too dark at this point. I darken the eye, remembering to leave the wet-looking highlight white. I remind myself that the eye is like a sphere and use tiny strokes that follow the form of the sphere. I switch to an HB so I can outline the rigid beak. I put some tone in the beak but leave it lighter on the upper part to show the light hitting it.

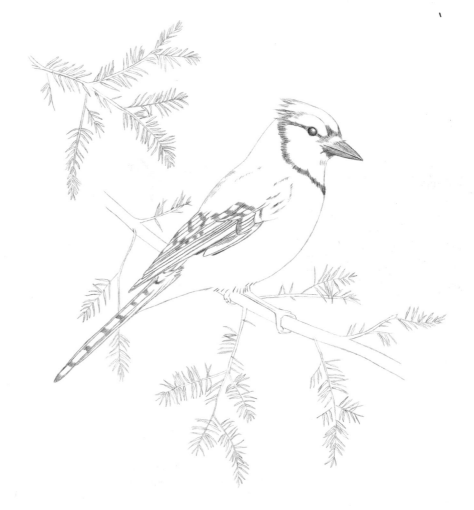

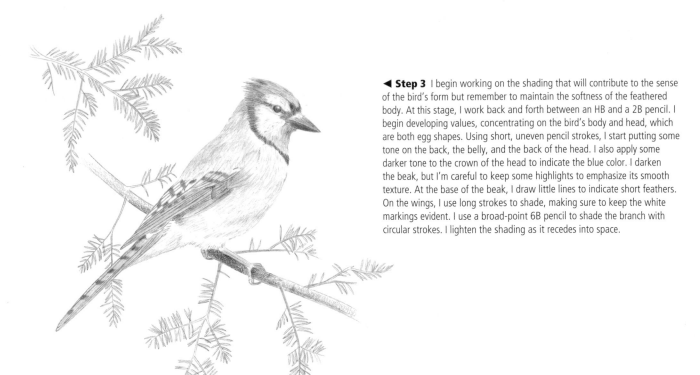

◄ **Step 3** I begin working on the shading that will contribute to the sense of the bird's form but remember to maintain the softness of the feathered body. At this stage, I work back and forth between an HB and a 2B pencil. I begin developing values, concentrating on the bird's body and head, which are both egg shapes. Using short, uneven pencil strokes, I start putting some tone on the back, the belly, and the back of the head. I also apply some darker tone to the crown of the head to indicate the blue color. I darken the beak, but I'm careful to keep some highlights to emphasize its smooth texture. At the base of the beak, I draw little lines to indicate short feathers. On the wings, I use long strokes to shade, making sure to keep the white markings evident. I use a broad-point 6B pencil to shade the branch with circular strokes. I lighten the shading as it recedes into space.

► **Step 4** It's important to balance the values of the form with the values of the color while keeping the textural elements intact. The form values are the values created by the light hitting the blue jay, whereas the color values are the ones representing the different colors of the actual bird. The texture emerges from the way these values are applied. In pencil, white is expressed as light shading, blue is the midtone, and black is the darkest shading. If I run into a conflict between the form and color values, I give priority to the form values. Now I deepen the black markings with short strokes of a sharp HB, leaving the white markings free of any tone. Where the feathers overlap and at the base of the tail and under the wings, I apply a deeper shade to indicate a shadow using the side of a 2B pencil. I add more shading to the head with short lines, and at the back of the crown I use longer lines for the sharply protruding feathers. Then I deepen the tone on the back and the belly. I leave a few little lines that extend beyond the edge of the bird, producing the feathered texture.

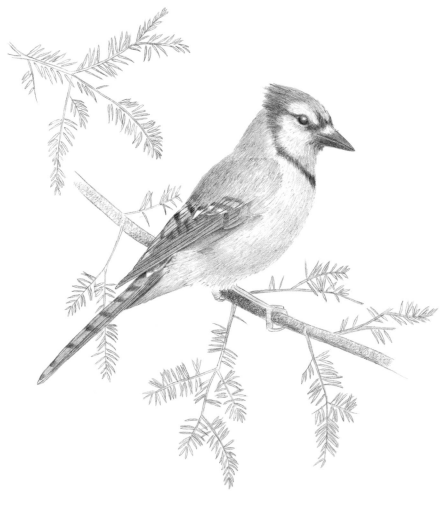

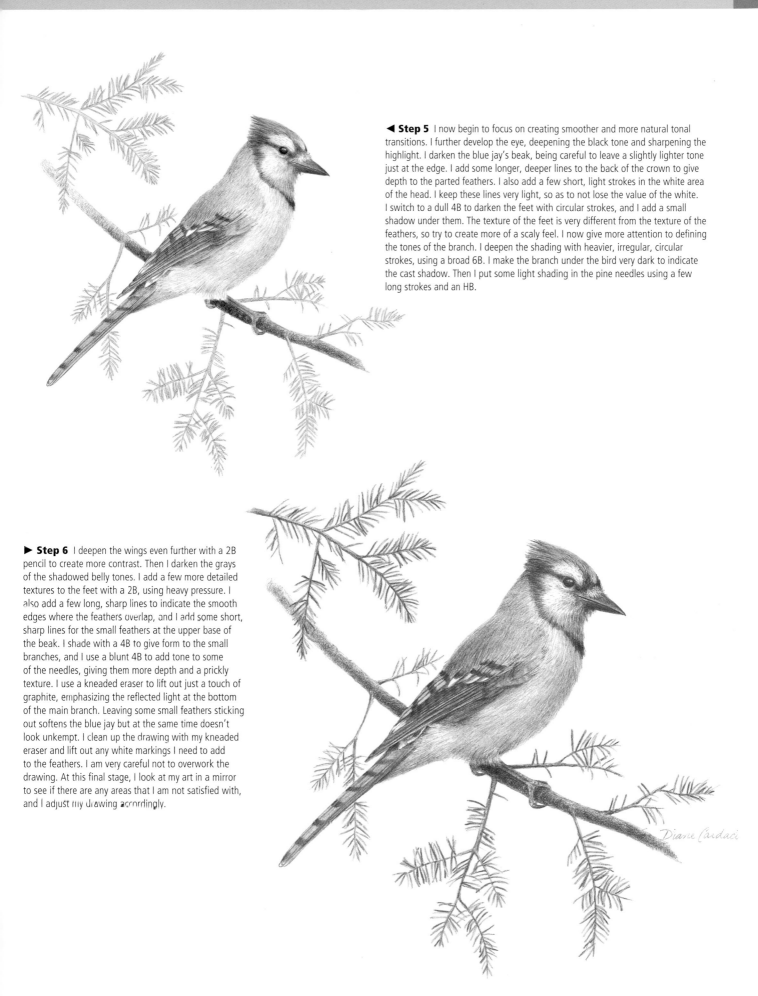

◄ Step 5 I now begin to focus on creating smoother and more natural tonal transitions. I further develop the eye, deepening the black tone and sharpening the highlight. I darken the blue jay's beak, being careful to leave a slightly lighter tone just at the edge. I add some longer, deeper lines to the back of the crown to give depth to the parted feathers. I also add a few short, light strokes in the white area of the head. I keep these lines very light, so as to not lose the value of the white. I switch to a dull 4B to darken the feet with circular strokes, and I add a small shadow under them. The texture of the feet is very different from the texture of the feathers, so try to create more of a scaly feel. I now give more attention to defining the tones of the branch. I deepen the shading with heavier, irregular, circular strokes, using a broad 6B. I make the branch under the bird very dark to indicate the cast shadow. Then I put some light shading in the pine needles using a few long strokes and an HB.

► Step 6 I deepen the wings even further with a 2B pencil to create more contrast. Then I darken the grays of the shadowed belly tones. I add a few more detailed textures to the feet with a 2B, using heavy pressure. I also add a few long, sharp lines to indicate the smooth edges where the feathers overlap, and I add some short, sharp lines for the small feathers at the upper base of the beak. I shade with a 4B to give form to the small branches, and I use a blunt 4B to add tone to some of the needles, giving them more depth and a prickly texture. I use a kneaded eraser to lift out just a touch of graphite, emphasizing the reflected light at the bottom of the main branch. Leaving some small feathers sticking out softens the blue jay but at the same time doesn't look unkempt. I clean up the drawing with my kneaded eraser and lift out any white markings I need to add to the feathers. I am very careful not to overwork the drawing. At this final stage, I look at my art in a mirror to see if there are any areas that I am not satisfied with, and I adjust my drawing accordingly.

LANDSCAPE TEXTURES

When there are a lot of trees, rocks, and other natural elements in a landscape, it can seem overwhelming to try to capture all of the textures. To simplify the process, I start by mapping out the major masses of the landscape elements, breaking them down into more manageable shapes. Then I can add other textural aspects, such as clouds and water, which bring the scene to life.

Land

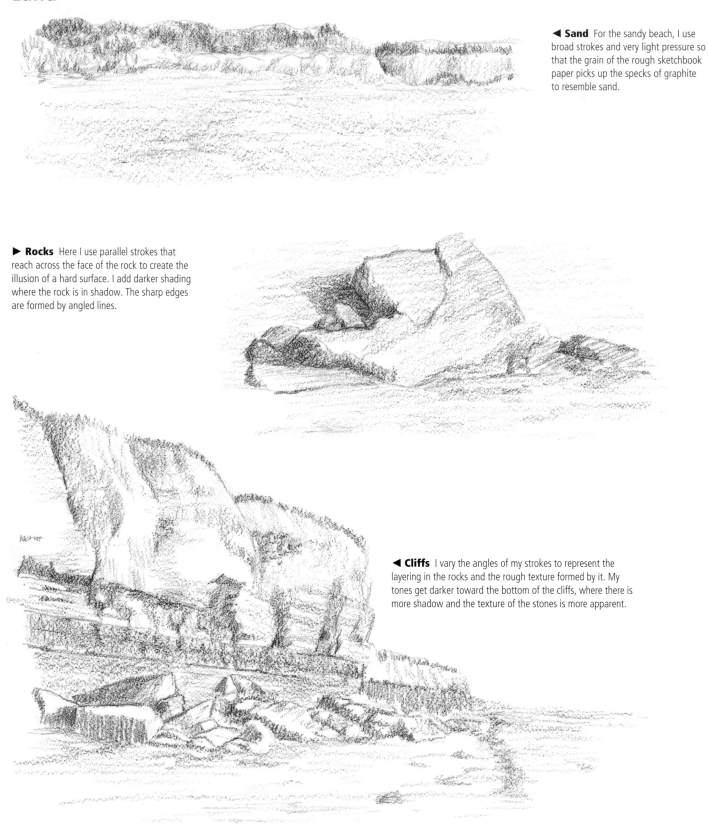

◀ **Sand** For the sandy beach, I use broad strokes and very light pressure so that the grain of the rough sketchbook paper picks up the specks of graphite to resemble sand.

▶ **Rocks** Here I use parallel strokes that reach across the face of the rock to create the illusion of a hard surface. I add darker shading where the rock is in shadow. The sharp edges are formed by angled lines.

◀ **Cliffs** I vary the angles of my strokes to represent the layering in the rocks and the rough texture formed by it. My tones get darker toward the bottom of the cliffs, where there is more shadow and the texture of the stones is more apparent.

Clouds

Cumulus For fluffy clouds, I dab my eraser gently for light gray areas and use more pressure to lift out the whites.

Cirrus To draw these wispy clouds, I lift out using a curving motion and then extend that motion horizontally.

Cumulonimbus To capture these dark storm clouds, I dab the graphite with my eraser; then I add dark tone and blend.

Water

Still Water When the air is perfectly still, water can appear almost like a mirror, reflecting objects clearly. To make the reflections evident, I use dense, dark strokes.

Rougher Water Here I deliberately allow the lines to be more wavy than in the previous example. I lift out with long, horizontal strokes. No reflections can be seen.

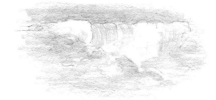

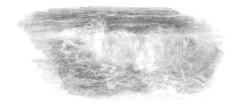

Waves Waves produce a sense of movement through frothy white caps. I start with the shape of the wave, create the darker parts of the water with a 4B, and blend.

I create a few white lines in the dark tone with my eraser, showing the building white caps. I dab the eraser to create the spray and lift out wavy shapes to make the foam.

Trees

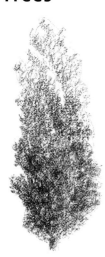

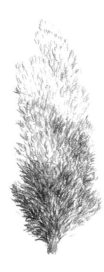

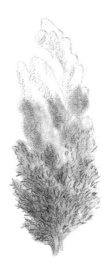

Painterly Strokes I use a wide, soft lead to lay down large, dense areas of tone. Finishing with some shorter strokes, I stipple to create detail and add texture. This gives a tree an open, leafy pattern.

Linear Strokes I use a sharper pencil and small, thin strokes. I vary the direction and density of my lines to develop the dark and light values that establish the form of the tree. This technique is ideal for prickly pine trees.

Combining Techniques I put down some tone and then smear it with a blending stump. Then I use short, linear strokes with a sharp pencil to create the texture. This creates a tree with a softer-looking texture.

LAKE SCENE

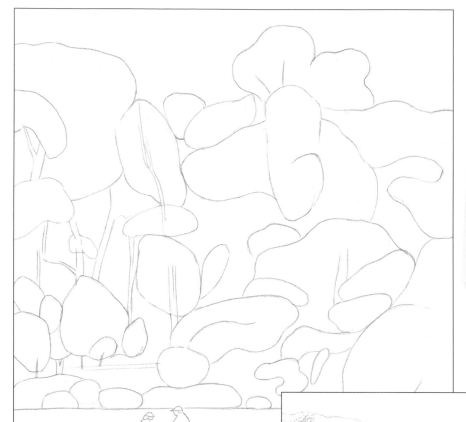

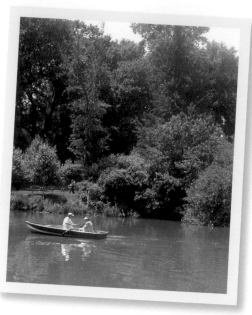

▲ **Taking Artistic License** You have the freedom to change elements of your photo references. Here I changed the direction of the boat, which I thought would improve the composition.

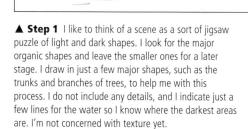

▲ **Step 1** I like to think of a scene as a sort of jigsaw puzzle of light and dark shapes. I look for the major organic shapes and leave the smaller ones for a later stage. I draw in just a few major shapes, such as the trunks and branches of trees, to help me with this process. I do not include any details, and I indicate just a few lines for the water so I know where the darkest areas are. I'm not concerned with texture yet.

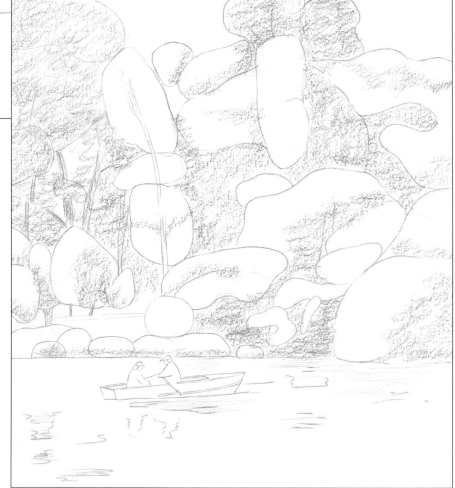

▶ **Step 2** Using the side of a 6B pencil, I lay in tone for the large masses of foliage. I do not worry too much about being exact. I use long strokes to put some tone on the trunks. Then I switch to the side of an HB and very lightly put down some preliminary tone in horizontal strokes to show the calm water.

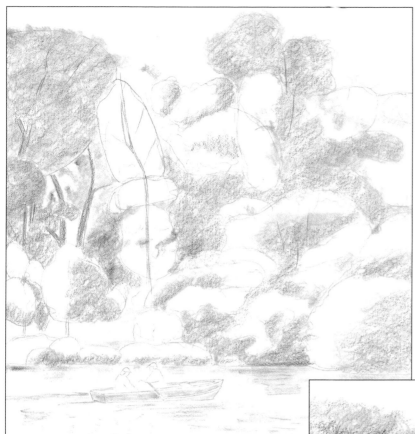

◄ **Step 3** I continue the process of developing the masses, but now I use a thick blending stump, blending the textures that are indistinct in the background. I think of myself as painting more than drawing, creating a wash effect by loosely smearing the tones I have already put down for the foliage. I use circular strokes and keep them very free, not worrying about the outlines. I use long strokes with the stump on the main trunks and branches, and then I use a sharp HB to create the hard edges that better define their texture. For the water, I dip my stump into some carbon dust and apply it to the darker areas of the water, using long, free, horizontal strokes. I switch to a thin stump and apply a "wash" to the boat.

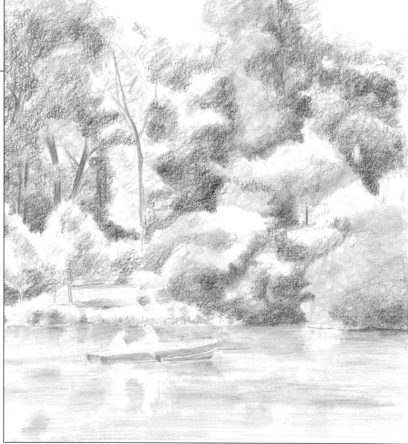

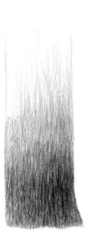

▲ **Creating Bark** I use the side of a 2B to shade the bark of the trees, varying my lines so the patterns aren't rigid. Once the tone is built up, I go back and accentuate the grooves with the point of my pencil. Then I lift out with my eraser. The more range you create between the lightest and darkest tones, the rougher the bark will appear.

▲ **Step 4** Now I start defining the shapes and textures of the foliage masses. Using a 6B, I go back in with loose strokes and put more tone in the darker, smaller masses. I break down the light and dark areas and refine their shapes. For the water, I use the side of an HB, allowing my hand to create slight waves in the lines. I add another layer of carbon dust with my stump where the tonal variations occur in the water.

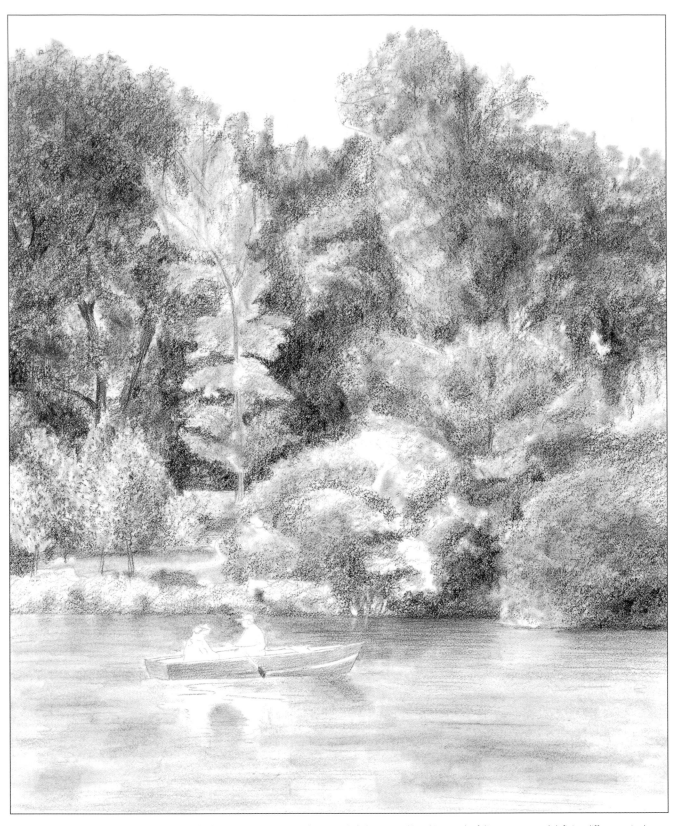

Step 5 At this point, I begin to work back and forth between my stump and 6B pencil, darkening and breaking up the foliage masses and defining differences in the textures they create. I continue to work very freely, allowing accidental effects to create more atmosphere. I use a sharp 2B to lightly put branches in the tree masses that are closest to the sky. With heavier pressure, I put some additional branches in the foliage masses. For the small trees near the water, I use a 6B to stipple, showing the leafy textures and creating more stippling where the form turns away from the light. I repeat the same process I used earlier for the water and darken the shadowy areas. I use the deepest tone along the bank, leaving some areas lighter based on the shape and textural quality of the reflections.

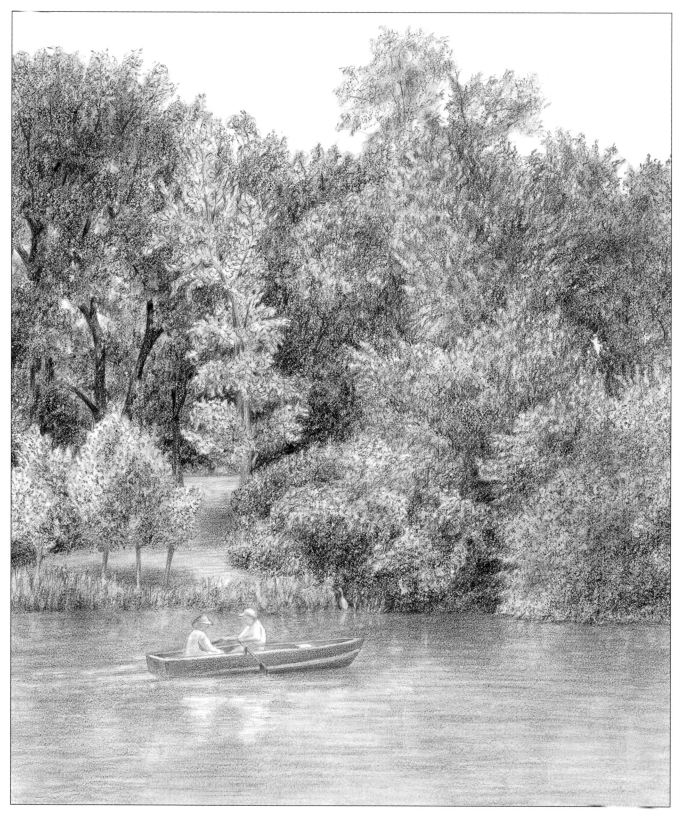

Step 6 Now the forms are well established, and the interaction of the paper with my loose strokes has created a good basis of texture. The sleek sides of the boat are shaded more heavily. Next I use more deliberate strokes to create different types of textures within the trees. I lightly stipple along the branches that extend into the sky to create an illusion of leaves; I use the 2B to put in a few more branches; and I draw some small, curved strokes with a 4B, adding individual texture to the trees. For the grassy area, I use the stump and add a few pencil strokes. I use my kneaded eraser to pick out additional lights in the foliage, boat, and water, helping emphasize the darks. I carefully define the shape of the bird by the shore and the trunks of the small trees with the sharp point of an HB. I don't want to create too much detail on the people, so I add just a little shading.

ANIMAL TEXTURES

Once you've mastered the subtleties of rendering fur and hair textures, you'll be able to draw a whole zoo full of animals! Animals are more than their coats, however; for example, a dog has a wide array of textures to experiment with, from the shining eyes to the wet nose.

Fur and Hair

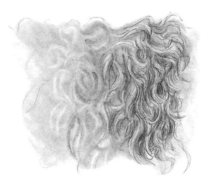

▲ **Curly** I create a base tone using carbon dust and a stump. Then I lift out long, curly, white lines to achieve the kinky texture of the hair. I add curly lines on top of the white areas with a very sharp HB pencil.

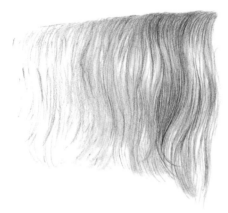

▲ **Silky** I outline the prominent hair patterns with an HB and then put in some tone with strokes that follow the gentle waves of the hair. Then I use an eraser to pick out shiny highlights.

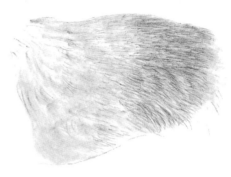

▲ **Short and Wiry** I put down some carbon dust and blend with a stump, using short strokes when blending. I draw short lines to develop the hair growth patterns and make slight changes to the direction of individual hairs to produce the wiry texture.

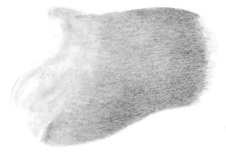

▲ **Short and Smooth** I lay in tone using carbon dust. Then I make several very short strokes with the side of a 2B pencil to achieve the smooth-textured appearance.

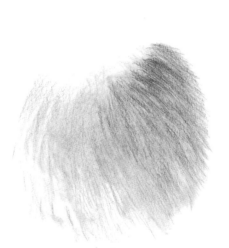

▲ **Long and Fluffy** I put down my base tone, then add some long, slightly curved, light strokes with the side of a 2B. On top of that, I put in thin lines with the point of the pencil and add some heavier lines where the hair is darker.

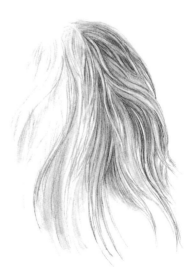

▲ **Long and Smooth** I draw long, wavy lines, then add tone with carbon dust. I alternate shading with the side of the pencil, drawing fine lines with the point of an HB, and lifting out white areas with an eraser to get the soft look.

YORKSHIRE TERRIER

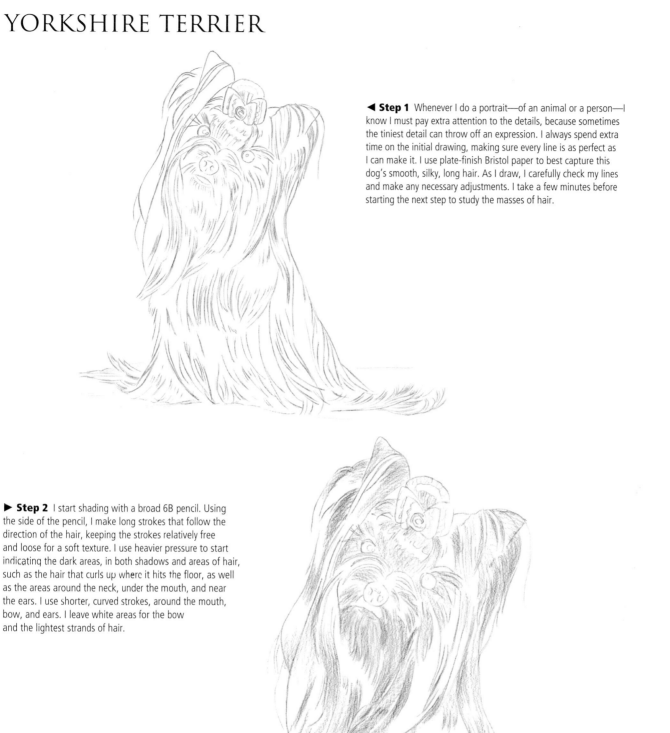

◄ **Step 1** Whenever I do a portrait—of an animal or a person—I know I must pay extra attention to the details, because sometimes the tiniest detail can throw off an expression. I always spend extra time on the initial drawing, making sure every line is as perfect as I can make it. I use plate-finish Bristol paper to best capture this dog's smooth, silky, long hair. As I draw, I carefully check my lines and make any necessary adjustments. I take a few minutes before starting the next step to study the masses of hair.

▶ **Step 2** I start shading with a broad 6B pencil. Using the side of the pencil, I make long strokes that follow the direction of the hair, keeping the strokes relatively free and loose for a soft texture. I use heavier pressure to start indicating the dark areas, in both shadows and areas of hair, such as the hair that curls up where it hits the floor, as well as the areas around the neck, under the mouth, and near the ears. I use shorter, curved strokes, around the mouth, bow, and ears. I leave white areas for the bow and the lightest strands of hair.

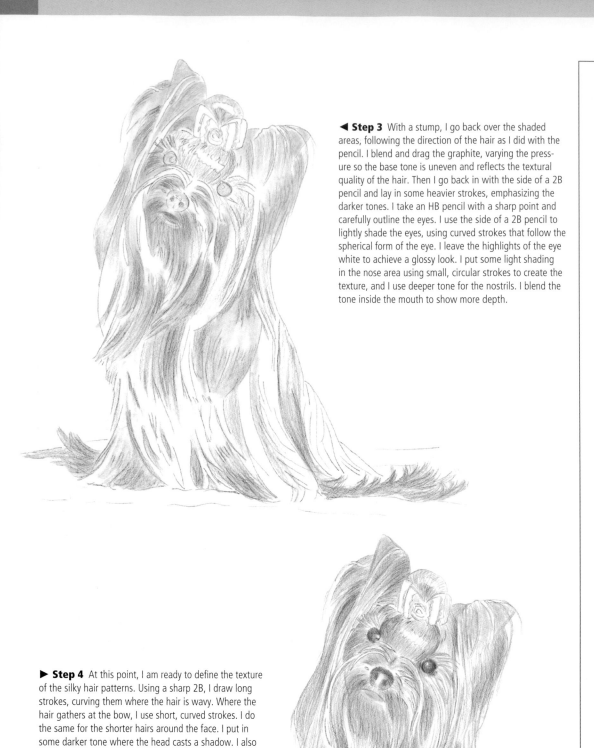

◄ Step 3 With a stump, I go back over the shaded areas, following the direction of the hair as I did with the pencil. I blend and drag the graphite, varying the pressure so the base tone is uneven and reflects the textural quality of the hair. Then I go back in with the side of a 2B pencil and lay in some heavier strokes, emphasizing the darker tones. I take an HB pencil with a sharp point and carefully outline the eyes. I use the side of a 2B pencil to lightly shade the eyes, using curved strokes that follow the spherical form of the eye. I leave the highlights of the eye white to achieve a glossy look. I put some light shading in the nose area using small, circular strokes to create the texture, and I use deeper tone for the nostrils. I blend the tone inside the mouth to show more depth.

► Step 4 At this point, I am ready to define the texture of the silky hair patterns. Using a sharp 2B, I draw long strokes, curving them where the hair is wavy. Where the hair gathers at the bow, I use short, curved strokes. I do the same for the shorter hairs around the face. I put in some darker tone where the head casts a shadow. I also darken the hair along the left side of the face; this helps define the softness of the long, lighter hairs draped over the ear. Next, with the side of an HB, I add deep shading around the edge of the eyes. For the nose, I continue to use circular strokes to deepen the value while maintaining the distinct texture. Then I use my eraser to lift out some highlights in the hair.

Canine Eyes

Eyes are the windows to the soul. It's important to draw them with plenty of expression. A dog's eye is different than a human's, so pay close attention to the tones you use.

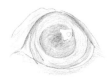

Step 1 I outline the eye; then I use circular strokes to create a base tone. I put darker shading in the center of the iris for the pupil, as well as around the outer edge. I leave the square-shaped highlight white.

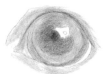

Step 2 Next I deepen the tone in the pupil, around the outside of the iris, and along the eyelids. The contrast of the dark pupil against the white highlight makes the highlight appear even brighter.

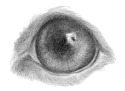

Step 3 I maintain a sharp edge for the highlight, which gives the eye a wet, glossy look. I shade around the eyes using short strokes with the side of the pencil; then I draw a few hairs around the eye with a sharp point.

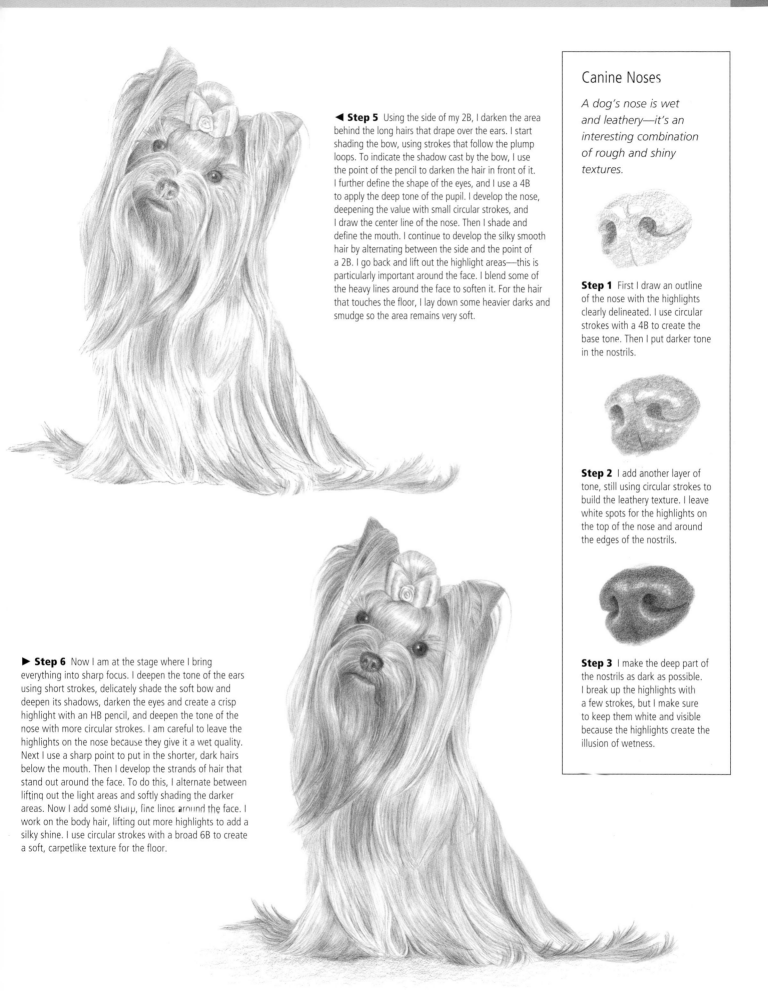

◄ Step 5 Using the side of my 2B, I darken the area behind the long hairs that drape over the ears. I start shading the bow, using strokes that follow the plump loops. To indicate the shadow cast by the bow, I use the point of the pencil to darken the hair in front of it. I further define the shape of the eyes, and I use a 4B to apply the deep tone of the pupil. I develop the nose, deepening the value with small circular strokes, and I draw the center line of the nose. Then I shade and define the mouth. I continue to develop the silky smooth hair by alternating between the side and the point of a 2B. I go back and lift out the highlight areas—this is particularly important around the face. I blend some of the heavy lines around the face to soften it. For the hair that touches the floor, I lay down some heavier darks and smudge so the area remains very soft.

Canine Noses

A dog's nose is wet and leathery—it's an interesting combination of rough and shiny textures.

Step 1 First I draw an outline of the nose with the highlights clearly delineated. I use circular strokes with a 4B to create the base tone. Then I put darker tone in the nostrils.

Step 2 I add another layer of tone, still using circular strokes to build the leathery texture. I leave white spots for the highlights on the top of the nose and around the edges of the nostrils.

Step 3 I make the deep part of the nostrils as dark as possible. I break up the highlights with a few strokes, but I make sure to keep them white and visible because the highlights create the illusion of wetness.

► Step 6 Now I am at the stage where I bring everything into sharp focus. I deepen the tone of the ears using short strokes, delicately shade the soft bow and deepen its shadows, darken the eyes and create a crisp highlight with an HB pencil, and deepen the tone of the nose with more circular strokes. I am careful to leave the highlights on the nose because they give it a wet quality. Next I use a sharp point to put in the shorter, dark hairs below the mouth. Then I develop the strands of hair that stand out around the face. To do this, I alternate between lifting out the light areas and softly shading the darker areas. Now I add some sharp, fine lines around the face. I work on the body hair, lifting out more highlights to add a silky shine. I use circular strokes with a broad 6B to create a soft, carpetlike texture for the floor.

PORTRAIT TEXTURES

Capturing a likeness can be one of the greatest challenges for an artist, yet it also can be incredibly rewarding. Careful observation, coupled with a thorough understanding of the form of the head, is the foundation of a successful portrait. Consideration must be given to how the light flows over the head and facial features, as well as the very different textures of hair, teeth, skin, and eyes.

Hair

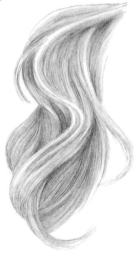

◄ **Light and Wavy** Carbon dust and a stump create a base of light, subtle tone. I add long, flowing lines, following the soft waves of the hair. The strands in the foreground stay very light to emphasize the color of the hair.

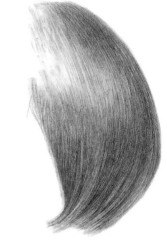

◄ **Dark and Straight** First I outline the sculptured shape of this hairstyle and then apply a layer of carbon dust. Because the hair is so sleek, there is a strong band of highlights. I apply even tone with long, curved strokes and a 2B.

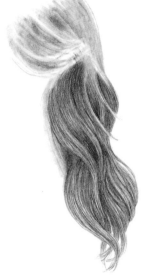

► **Dark and Wavy** I draw the main, curving hair forms; layer in some carbon dust; and draw wavy lines with the point of a 2B pencil. I use a 4B for the darkest darks and lift out the lighter, highlighted strands with a kneaded eraser.

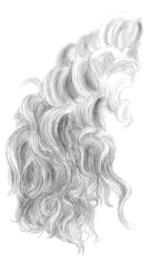

► **Light and Curly** I outline the main masses of curls and some individual hairs. Then I use a sharp HB to shade. I lay in some carbon dust for the hair that is in shadow. Then I lift out some highlights with curved strokes.

Fabrics

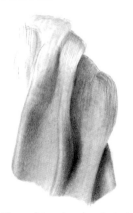

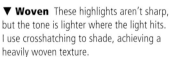

▼ **Woven** These highlights aren't sharp, but the tone is lighter where the light hits. I use crosshatching to shade, achieving a heavily woven texture.

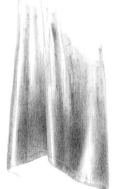

▼ **Lacework** This fabric is matte, so the tonal transitions are very soft with no bright highlights. I make the dark holes with a sharp 2B.

▲ **Flannel** I apply carbon dust using circular strokes. Then I layer in long strokes with a 2B and blend, keeping the highlights soft and subtle.

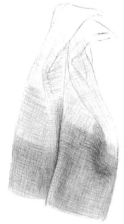

▲ **Satin** I draw the main folds, then apply a layer of carbon dust. I define the highlights with my eraser for shine, and I lift out for the stitches.

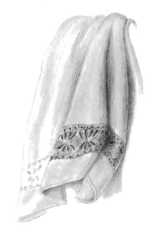

A YOUNG GIRL

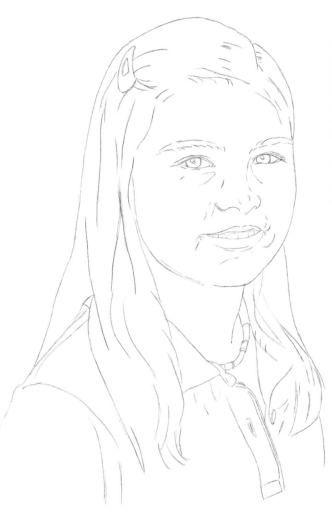

◀ **Step 1** When choosing the pose for a portrait, it is important to think about the qualities that are particularly special about your subject. This is an extremely sweet and energetic young lady, and I wanted to capture her personality in my portrait. I didn't want to draw her with a full smile because her eyes would be smaller and not as expressive. To reflect her love of sports, I chose to draw her in a polo shirt. I like to have my female subjects choose some jewelry because necklaces and bracelets offer additional textural interest. For portraits, I almost always use smooth Bristol paper, as it is best for capturing the subtle details. I use a sharp HB pencil for my outline of the basic features of the head. I check and recheck the accuracy of my drawing, because the slightest errors in observation will take away from the likeness of the subject.

▶ **Step 2** Using the side of a 2B pencil, I draw long, flowing strokes that follow the direction of her smooth, straight hair. I like to start with the hair because it helps me loosen up. Then I put very light tone in the iris of each eye, using small, circular strokes. Under the eyebrow of her left eye, I develop the shadow of this *down plane*—a plane that is angled down, even if only slightly, and therefore is often in shadow. For the side of the nose, I use longer strokes with a slight curve, but for the tip I think of a small sphere and use shorter, curved strokes. On the side of the face, I use very light strokes that curve with the shape of the face. I indicate the shadow directly under the lower lip. Then I draw lines that indicate the cylindrical shape of the neck, and I add some darker tone for the cast shadow under the collar.

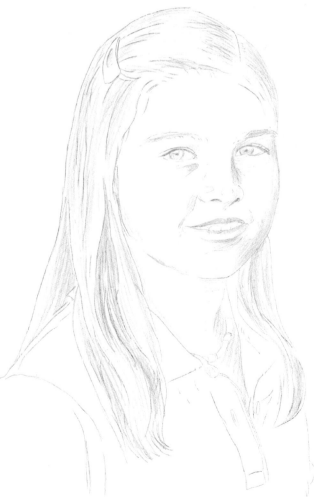

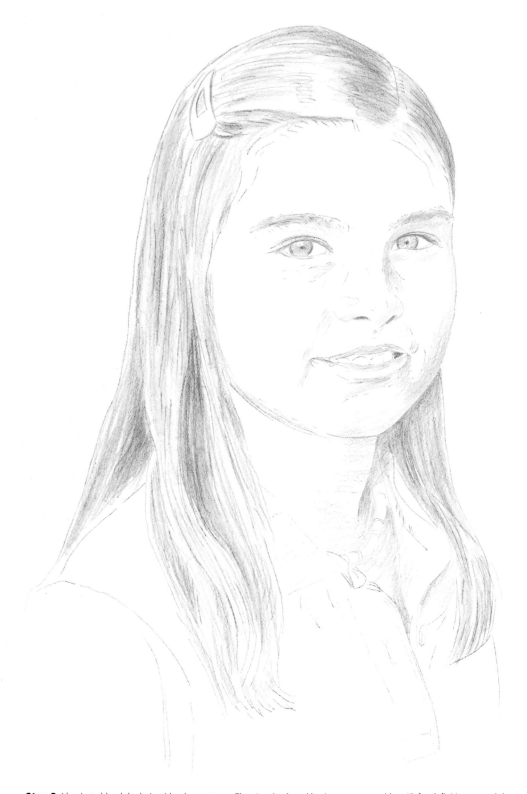

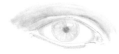
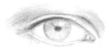

Step 3 I begin to blend the hair with a large stump. Then I go back and lay in more tone with a 4B for definition around the area where the hair parts and around the side of the face. With the lightest touch, I slightly blend the pencil strokes around the side of the face, being careful to follow the softly rounded contour of the cheeks. With a smaller stump, I lightly blend the areas around the eyes, mouth, nose, and eyebrows. I take my 2B pencil and put some deeper tone in the nostrils, the corner of the mouth, and the pupil of the eye. I darken the lines around the eye, making the line above the eye thicker to indicate the lashes. I work in light layers because it allows me to slowly develop the form. I study the subject as I draw, so by the time I start using deeper tones that would be more difficult to erase, I have a much greater understanding of the forms and shadows.

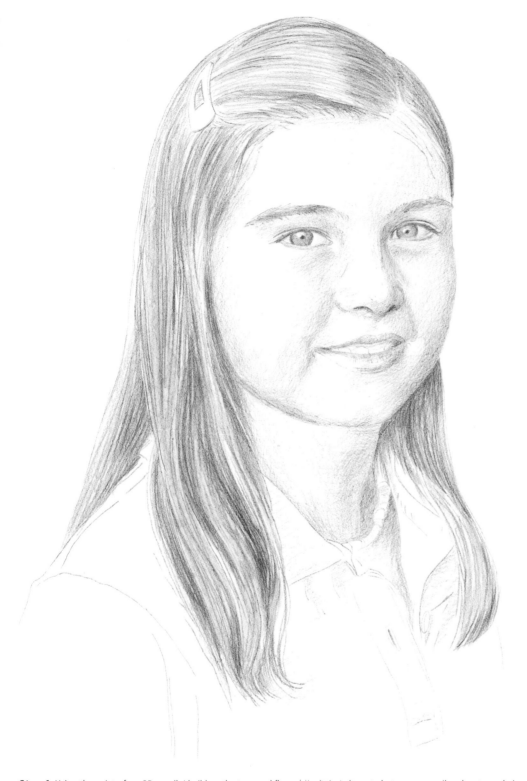

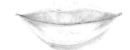

Rendering Lips

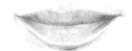

Step 1 I start with an outline of the mouth and apply light tone with carbon dust and a stump.

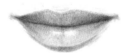

Step 2 I add another layer of tone with the carbon dust and darken underneath the bottom lip and in the corners of the mouth. I switch to an HB pencil and stroke outward with short, slightly curved lines, leaving white highlights.

Step 3 Now I use the side of the pencil to add more tone to the lips, lifting out the highlights. I use a 2B to draw the separation of the lips; then I add more contour lines with an HB. I add a touch of carbon dust to the corners of the mouth.

Step 4 Using the point of my 2B pencil, I build up the tone and flow of the hair. I alternate between a pencil and a stump, being careful to retain the highlights. I work on the face, using a delicate buildup of crosshatching. I draw very light, long strokes with an HB across the smooth skin of the forehead. I shade around the eye area, always following the contour of the form. I do the same for the nose, lips, cheeks, and chin, building up tone slowly. I put very subtle shading on the teeth—it is important not to make the teeth too white. I deepen the tone of the irises with a 2B, and I lift out to adjust the placement of the highlights. I move to the neck area, using heavy pressure in the cast shadow areas. I begin to shade the collar of the shirt, keeping my strokes farther apart to start developing a feel of the knit fabric. Then I use curved lines to indicate the necklace.

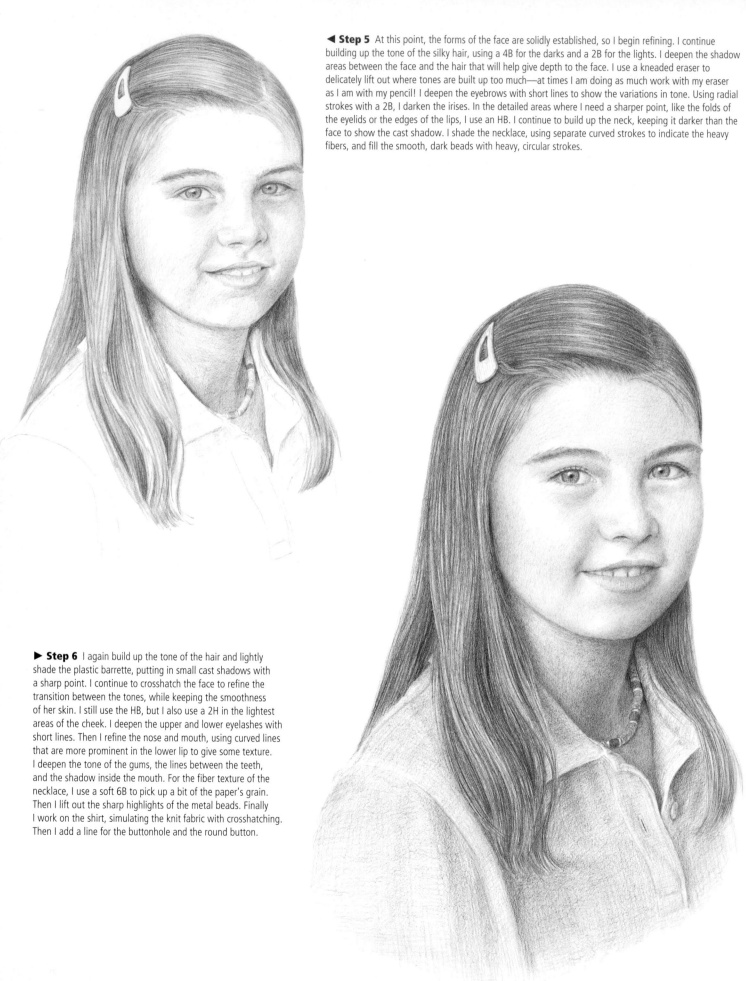

◄ Step 5 At this point, the forms of the face are solidly established, so I begin refining. I continue building up the tone of the silky hair, using a 4B for the darks and a 2B for the lights. I deepen the shadow areas between the face and the hair that will help give depth to the face. I use a kneaded eraser to delicately lift out where tones are built up too much—at times I am doing as much work with my eraser as I am with my pencil! I deepen the eyebrows with short lines to show the variations in tone. Using radial strokes with a 2B, I darken the irises. In the detailed areas where I need a sharper point, like the folds of the eyelids or the edges of the lips, I use an HB. I continue to build up the neck, keeping it darker than the face to show the cast shadow. I shade the necklace, using separate curved strokes to indicate the heavy fibers, and fill the smooth, dark beads with heavy, circular strokes.

► Step 6 I again build up the tone of the hair and lightly shade the plastic barrette, putting in small cast shadows with a sharp point. I continue to crosshatch the face to refine the transition between the tones, while keeping the smoothness of her skin. I still use the HB, but I also use a 2H in the lightest areas of the cheek. I deepen the upper and lower eyelashes with short lines. Then I refine the nose and mouth, using curved lines that are more prominent in the lower lip to give some texture. I deepen the tone of the gums, the lines between the teeth, and the shadow inside the mouth. For the fiber texture of the necklace, I use a soft 6B to pick up a bit of the paper's grain. Then I lift out the sharp highlights of the metal beads. Finally I work on the shirt, simulating the knit fabric with crosshatching. Then I add a line for the buttonhole and the round button.

CHAPTER 4

STEP-BY-STEP EXERCISES

with Carol Rosinski

Pencil drawing is the most simple and basic art form, yet the range of possible expressions is almost limitless. From energetic sketches of figures in action to simple studies of serene still lifes, drawing can capture time and movement, light and shadow, line, texture, and form—and so much more! As a pencil glides across paper, emotions can be recorded and memories preserved.

Drawing is affordable—a pencil, a piece of paper, and an eraser are all you need. And drawing is a skill that can easily be developed. Mastering the basic techniques is easier than you may imagine! With a willingness to learn and time to devote to practice, your efforts will be rewarded with a new way to express yourself!

—Carol Rosinski

About Carol Rosinski

Carol Rosinski has always drawn. From an early age, she could pick up and transform paper and graphite into a living scene with depth and texture. Carol enjoys working with graphite because she finds it so flexible and expressive. And she loves helping people explore graphite's potential, teaching them what their tools can accomplish to make drawing even more fun and exciting. Carol has worked as an illustrator, and her artwork has been shown in galleries and has appeared in a number of publications. She currently creates her art in the "wilds" of Michigan, where she lives with her husband and cats. She finds her inspiration there, surrounded by trees, birds, and all the wonders of nature.

TEDDY BEAR

Texture can be broken down into patterns of light and shadow, making the texture easier to reproduce on paper. When I draw a large textured area, I always use the same sequence of actions: hatch and blend the middle value of each area; hatch and blend the large shadow areas; pull out the large highlighted areas with an eraser; draw in the small and dark details; and use an eraser to pull out the smallest, lightest details. This step-by-step exercise will help you focus on replicating the soft fur of a teddy bear. You'll need 2B, B, and 2H pencils; a kneaded eraser; and small and large trimmed brushes for this project.

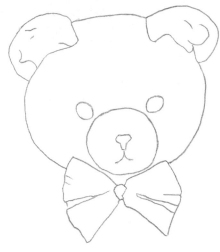

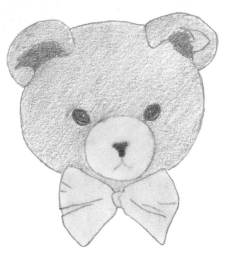

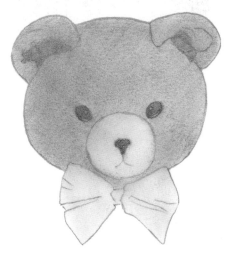

Step 1 Block in the basic outline of the subject using a B pencil with medium pressure, taking care not to dent or score the paper. Indicate the wrinkles in the ear as a guide for later details.

Step 2 Using medium pressure and a dull B pencil, hatch in the middle values of each area. Keep the values relative to one another.

Step 3 Stroke over the entire drawing and smooth it using different sized brushes. Use the small brush for little areas that require cleaner edges, and use the large brush, which doesn't require as much control of the bristles, for bigger areas.

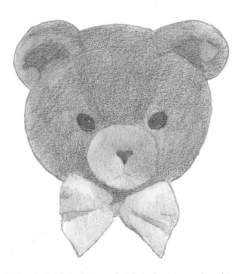

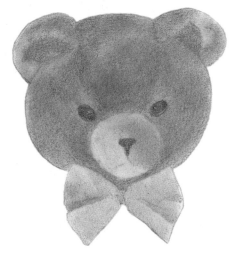

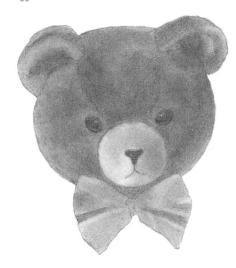

Step 4 Hatch in the large facial shadows to a value of 6 (see below) with a dull B pencil. Look only at the overall shadow shapes and exclude the darkest details. Perform the same process on the muzzle and bow, using a 2H pencil and very light pressure.

Step 5 Smooth the hatching again with a brush, blending just enough to produce a soft and fuzzy appearance, and allowing the slightly rough paper to do some of the work. Work the same way on the bow and muzzle, using very slight pressure on the brush.

Step 6 Shape your kneaded eraser to a rounded point to lift out highlights. If you lighten an area too much, re-darken it by rubbing the brush back and forth over the highlight.

Value Scale

Artist Carol Rosinski uses a slightly expanded value scale, so for the lessons in this chapter, please refer to the scale below.

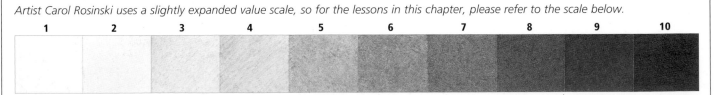

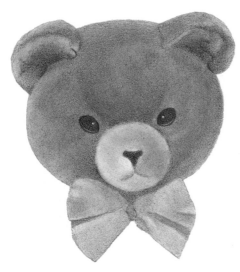

Step 7 Use a sharp 2B pencil to draw dark details, including the bear's eyes, nose, ears, and muzzle. Switch to a sharp B pencil to create the dark details on the muzzle and bow. To achieve these dark values, stroke over the soft areas with a sharp, hard pencil (see page 9). To finish, I carefully lighten the highlights under and in the eyes with a kneaded eraser pinched into a fine point.

Depicting Hard, Rough Textures

The world is full of fascinating textures, and you can replicate them all in pencil. As you've learned in this step-by-step lesson, the teddy bear's soft plush fur requires considerable blending and soft edges. However, the tree bark texture examples at right require more contrast in value and sharper lines. Experiment with your textural capabilities by attempting to re-create these rough textures.

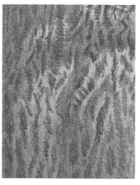

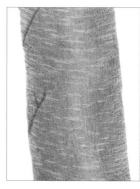

Ash Tree Bark Create the rough texture of this tree by drawing ragged ridges with dark, coarse strokes against a medium background.

Cherry Tree Bark Although this bark is much smoother and shows less contrast, the hard nature of the trunk is maintained by the crisp, defined edges.

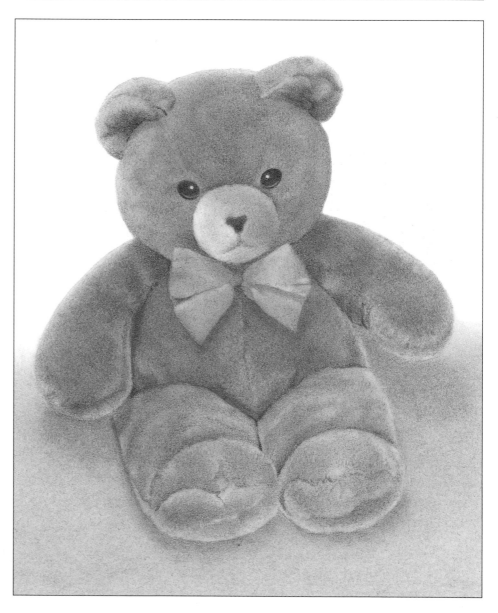

Step 8 Draw the rest of the plush body in the same manner as the head, starting with an outline and building up the values and textures in layers. The texture of the paper contributes to the plush look of this teddy bear. I chose cold-press watercolor paper with a slightly rough texture because the recessed areas of the paper catch the graphite, creating a pattern that mimics the soft, furry quality of the bear's plush material.

LANDSCAPE

To create this dramatic landscape scene, I used two photographic references: one that captures an interesting sky and one that presents a pleasing foreground. When I merge these elements, I achieve a better composition with a soft feel and subtle gradations in value. To best depict these qualities, I choose smooth paper without much texture.

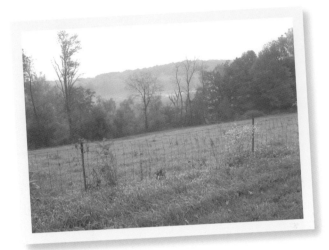

Capturing Contrasts I took this photo near Shavehead Lake in Michigan. It includes a range of values, textures, and lines—from the detailed foreground to the distant hill.

Pulling Out the Sky In this photo, taken from the same spot, I captured the drama of the sun veiled by sheets of soft clouds. I combined this photo and the one at left for my drawing.

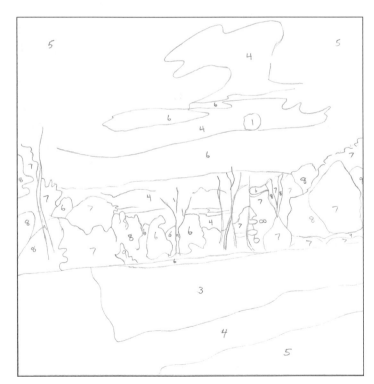

Step 1 Measure and frame the scene, roughing in a few details. Designate certain prominent trees to serve as reference points and also add the most obvious dark tree trunks. Then delineate the trees, meadow, and sky according to the differences in value. Once this "map" is in place, assign a number value to each section, using the value scale on page 122 as a reference.

Step 2 Mask the edges with tape to keep them clean and neat. Using loose graphite and a short, wide brush, fill in the entire sky area to a number 4 value. Brush the graphite down over the skyline and into the treetops, and smooth the sky with a tissue, avoiding the sun. Do the same for the meadow, working from a value number 5 in the bottom right and gradating to lighter values.

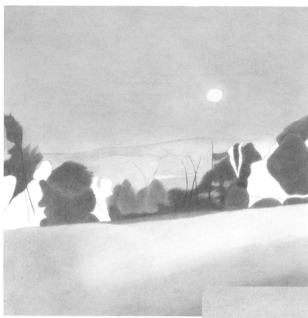

◀ **Step 3** Fill in the light- and middle-value trees using smooth hatching made with medium-soft pencils. Brush over the hatching after each layer to help even out the tone, repeating this process until each tree reaches the desired value. Then lightly rub the tree shapes with a tissue wrapped around your finger for an extra smooth texture.

▶ **Step 4** Using smooth hatching (see pages 8–9), fill in the darker tree shapes and smooth each area with a brush. Where two or more trees touch, darken one edge to push it back. Next brush loose graphite over the darkest parts of the drawing, repeating until you achieve the darkest value your paper allows.

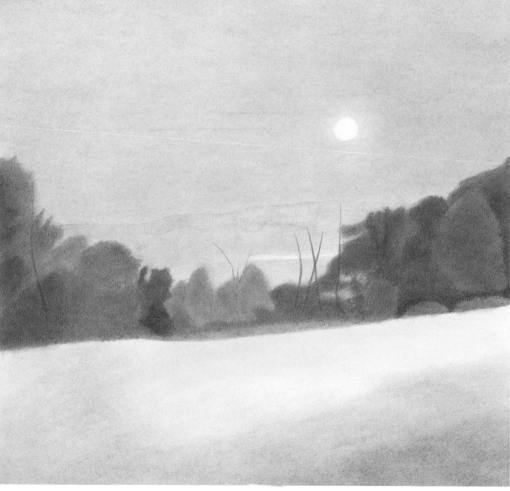

Pencil Key

Because pencil hardness varies from brand to brand, the exercises and projects in this chapter generically call for "hard" or "soft" pencils. Use the conversions at right to help determine which pencils to use in the projects of this chapter.

- Very hard: 4H–6H
- Hard: 3H–4H
- Medium hard: H–2H
- Medium: HB–F
- Medium soft: B–2B
- Soft: 3B–4B
- Very soft: 4B–6B

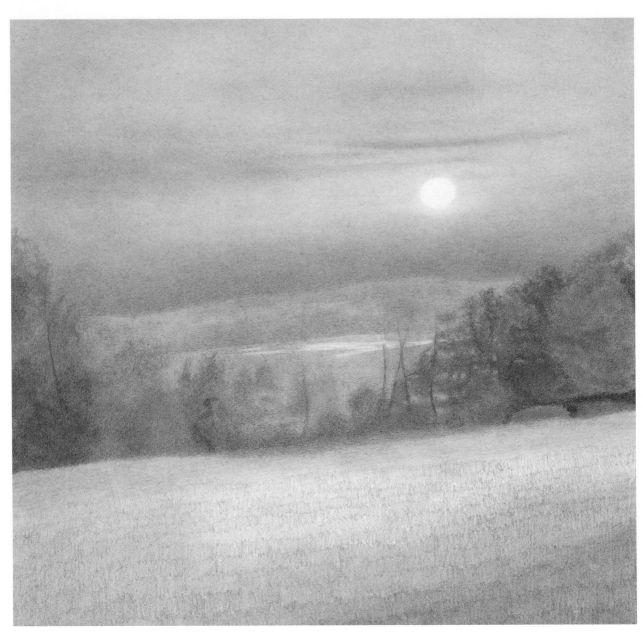

Step 5 Apply loose graphite with a brush, using horizontal strokes to darken the sky, and smooth out the graphite by sweeping a tissue in a horizontal motion over the entire area. Then darken the distant trees and swamp area to a number 5 value using a hard lead and horizontal hatching, taking care to leave the tops of some of the tree clumps lighter for easy identification in the next step. Darken the sky above the hills with a hard pencil to help separate the tree line from the sky. Using the point of a stick eraser, shape and lift out the water visible in the swamp area. Then pinch a kneaded eraser to a point and use it to lift out all the highlight areas of the middle-ground trees. Prepare the base for the grass texture in the foreground meadow by applying rough vertical hatching with a medium-soft pencil.

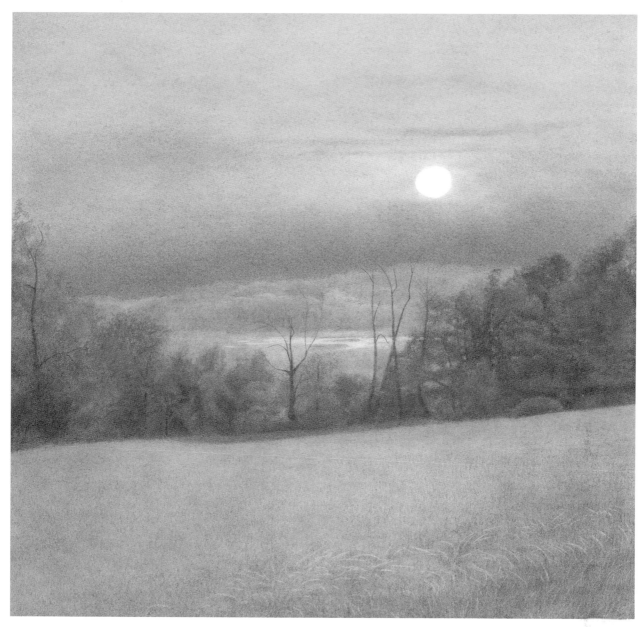

Step 6 Mottle the clouds using very hard pencils and a clean blending stump, and then complete the sun (see "Brightening the Sun" below). To further define the treetops, redraw the skyline with a series of scalloped strokes; then darken the branches and twigs (see "Creating Twigs" below). Soften the meadow by blending the hatching from step five using a stump held on its side. Using the point of a stick eraser, stroke blades of grass in the foreground; then add subtle shadows to the base of the clumps with a medium-soft lead.

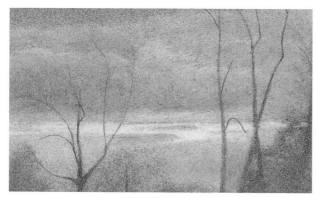

Creating Twigs To render the dark, thin lines of the tree branches, use a soft pencil honed to a sharp point.

Brightening the Sun To form the sun, pull out graphite with a kneaded eraser, leaving an imperfect circle for a realistic appearance through the clouds.

HORSE

This sturdy black horse has a playful but strong personality—one that I wanted to capture in this portrait. His mane falls on either side of his neck in twirling tendrils, providing an interesting contrast to his robust features. To render this abundance of textural details, I choose to work with watercolor paper that has a medium tooth, which will hold dark values and allow a supple look to be created for the coat.

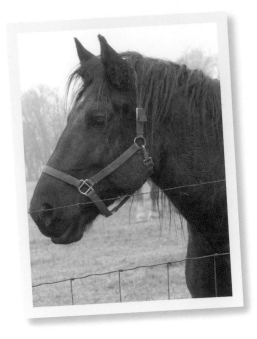

▶ **Distinguishing Values** I immediately take note that the values of the horse shown here are mostly dark, so there won't be much contrast. I make a conscious decision to lighten the mane a bit in my drawing, so the portrait doesn't become too monotonous.

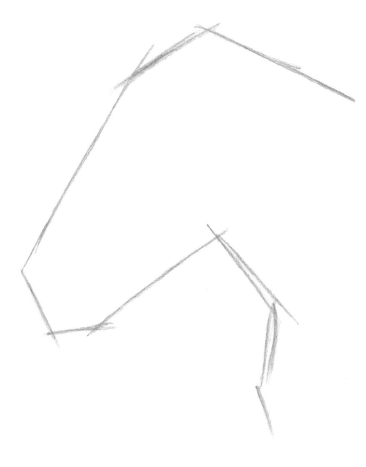

◀ **Step 1** First block in the general shape of the horse's profile on a large piece of paper, taking care to maintain the same proportions as the reference. Take a bit of artistic license and lengthen the back of the neck for balance.

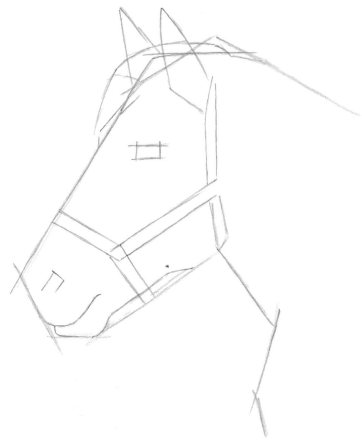

▶ **Step 2** Now indicate the eye, nose, mouth, and ears, constantly measuring and assessing the angles of each position; adjust them as you see fit. Then sketch the halter and define the shape of the chin and jaw. Add the brow ridge at left, noting how it angles away from the face; then draw the forelock (the hair between the ears).

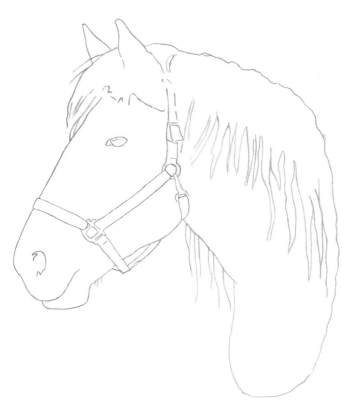

◄ Step 3 Using your initial blockings as a guide, refine the outlines of the eyes, nostrils, muzzle, and mane. Next focus on the halter, curving the lines of the straps slightly so they show the form of the horse's head. Then erase any initial guidelines that you no longer need. Draw the horse's mane, adding tendrils that taper to a point. Round off the neck with a long horseshoe shape that contrasts with the angular quality of the horse's profile.

► Step 4 Now transfer the drawing to a separate sheet of paper, and take note of the values based on the reference image. (You may want to use a photocopy of your drawing from step three instead.) Start by outlining the highlights and shadows on the horse's coat; then further delineate the variations in value. Next designate a value number to each area, using the value scale on page 122 for reference.

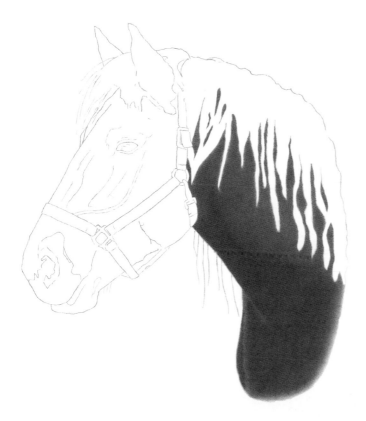

◄ Step 5 Return to your original drawing and use a medium-soft pencil to fill in the lighter value in the horse's neck and a soft pencil to add the darker value. Hatch the area, and then smooth the hatching with a brush. Repeat those steps until each area reaches the desired value. Where the neck joins the body, lighten the hatching to delineate the area.

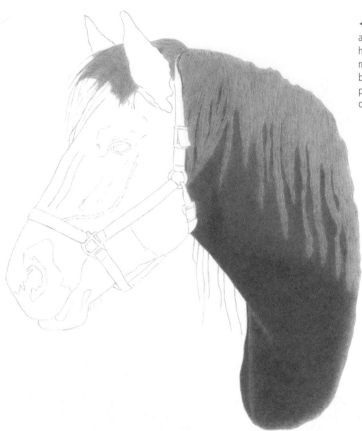

◀ **Step 6** Use a medium-hard pencil to fill in the mane. Apply varied long and short parallel strokes, deliberately leaving visible streaks within the vertical hatching to create a base for the mane's texture. Fill in the forelock in the same manner. Because hair like this is made up of rough light and dark strokes that blend together to make the value, it's a good idea to practice on a separate piece of paper that has the same texture as your final drawing; that way, you can determine what grade of pencil and combination of strokes will work best.

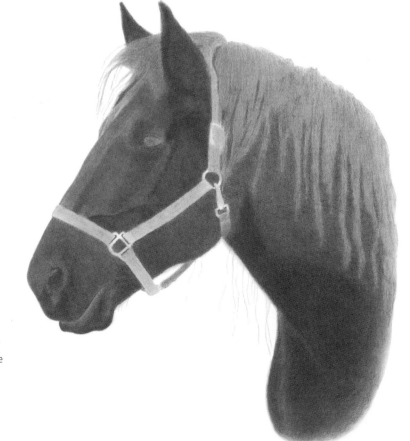

▶ **Step 7** Fill in each value area with hatching and smooth it out with a brush until it matches the desired value. If a value becomes too dark in an area, use a kneaded eraser to pull out the graphite. Round the extension of the neck even more and continue to fade the edge. Pull out highlights in the metal parts of the halter with a kneaded eraser.

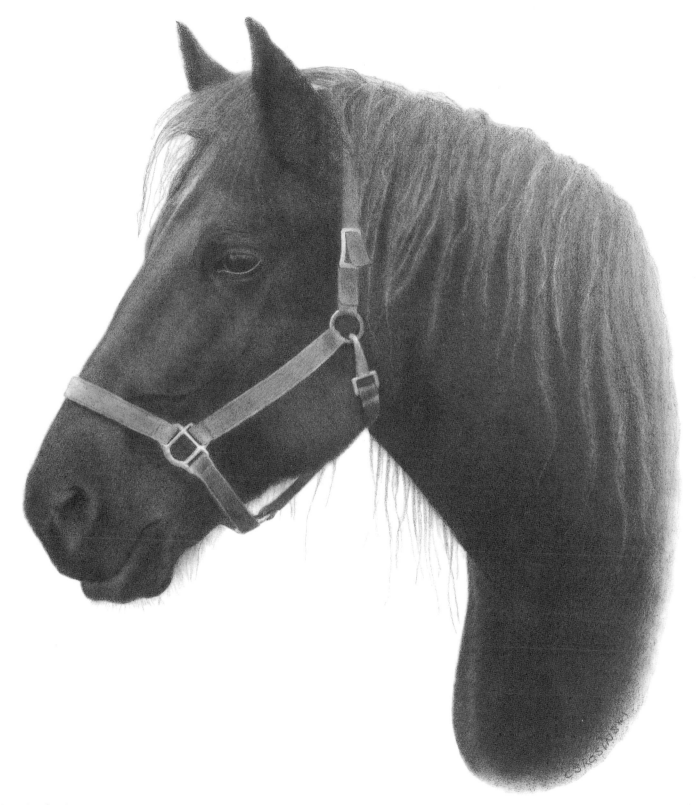

Step 8 Soften the texture on the cheek and neck, blending to draw more attention to the wispy mane. Then pull the medium-hard pencil over the mane with long strokes that follow the line of each twisting strand, making some areas darker for variations in depth. To finish the mane, add twisting highlights to some of the strands of hair, using a stick eraser cut into a point. Darken the far strands of hair and add a bit of fuzz on the horse's chin. Add the final details, including the shadows and stitching on the halter.

FLORAL STILL LIFE

When creating a flower arrangement, it's important to follow the rules of effective composition that you learned in Chapter 2. I place the vase slightly to the left to avoid a stagnant, overly symmetrical organization of the elements. Then I curve draped fabric or tissue paper around the base of the vase, bringing it off the opposite edge of the composition to lead the viewer's eye into the drawing. To give an informal touch to a classic subject, I lay some flowers on the table. Finally, I drape fabric in the background to create interesting folds and curves in the negative space.

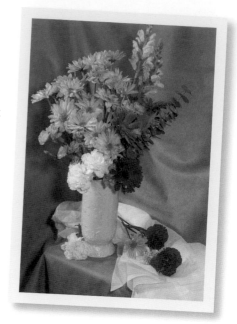

▶ **Creating Large Areas of Texture** For a mixed floral arrangement, I choose paper with a medium-rough texture; the tooth helps create interest within the large fabric background and makes the leaf and petal textures easier to render.

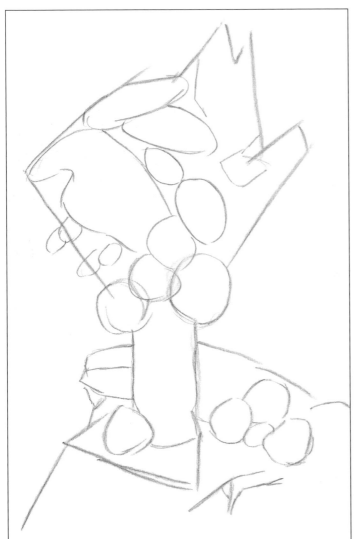

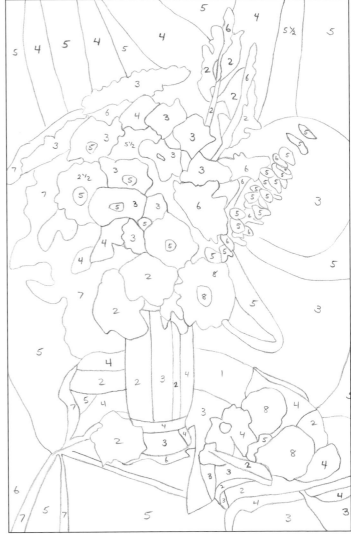

Step 1 For a complicated subject like this floral arrangement, block in the basic shapes of the largest objects before adding the smaller elements. To establish accurate proportions, use the vase as a reference for measurement. (In this case, the main bunch of flowers measures 1-3/4 vases high and wide.) Then loosely sketch the corner of the table and some of the large flower shapes within the bouquet and on the table.

Step 2 Add the rest of the flowers by simplifying their forms, indicating only a general outline—you will add details later. After outlining every object, erase any initial sketchmarks you don't need. Then transfer the outline (or make a photocopy) and break each object down into values. Create a "map" on a separate sheet of paper, referencing the value scale on page 122 to assign a value number to each area.

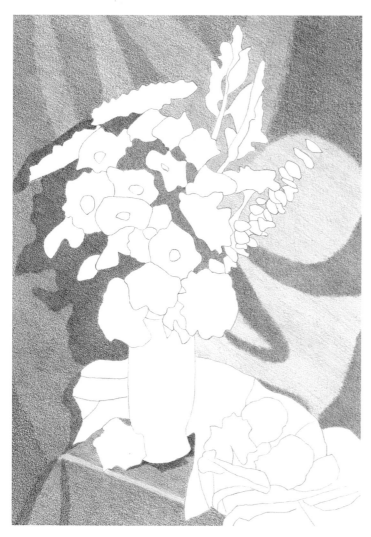

Step 3 To protect the edges of your drawing from smudges of graphite, mask the edges with tape. Then use a soft lead to lay down the hatching in values that correspond with your "map." Crosshatch the darkest shadows first; then add a layer of hatching over the entire background to unify the darks and lights.

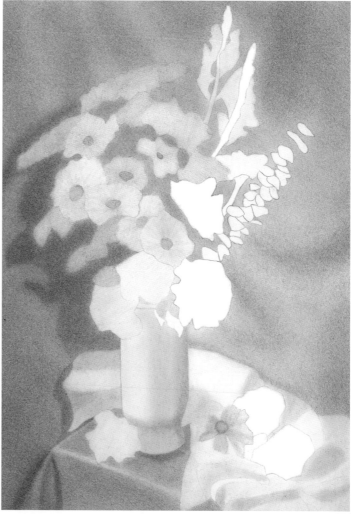

Step 4 Smooth the entire background with a tissue until it creates a soft texture. To work in the negative space between the flowers, fold the tissue several times and use one thick, pointed corner to smooth the hatching. After blending with the tissue to create a soft, shadowy effect, the cross-hatched shadows remain darker than the single-hatched areas. Hatch the light flowers with a medium-hard pencil, following the shape of the flower's petals; for instance, apply the hatching on the daisies with strokes that radiate out from the center, as the petals do. Add the flower centers with a softer lead; then add values to the vase and tissue paper on the table using a brush and loose graphite.

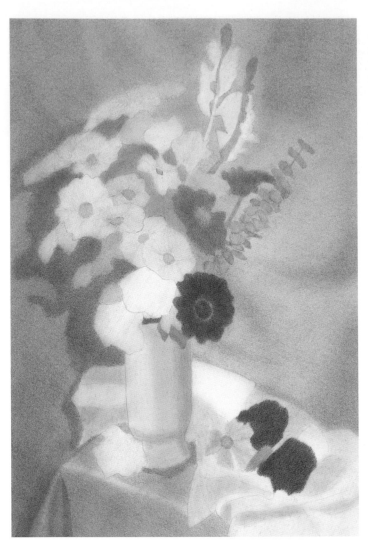

◄ Step 5 Now add the middle- and dark-value leaves and flowers. Begin by hatching the stem and leaves on the right with a medium-soft pencil, blending with a brush for a soft, even value. Next apply horizontal hatching with a soft pencil over the carnations and the dark daisies; then blend the strokes with a brush. If any lights are lost in the blending process, pull them out with a kneaded eraser.

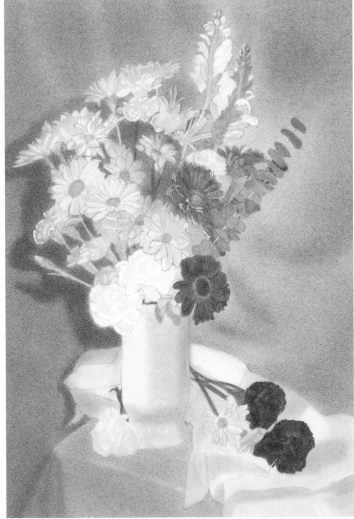

► Step 6 Now that you've established the basic value pattern, begin to add detail and give form to the elements. Shape the petals of the flowers by drawing into the edges of the flower shapes or by using a stick eraser to "push out" edges. Then use the same eraser to lift out highlights on the petals, as well as to pull out stems from the background. Use a medium-hard pencil to add more accents to the petals and flower centers.

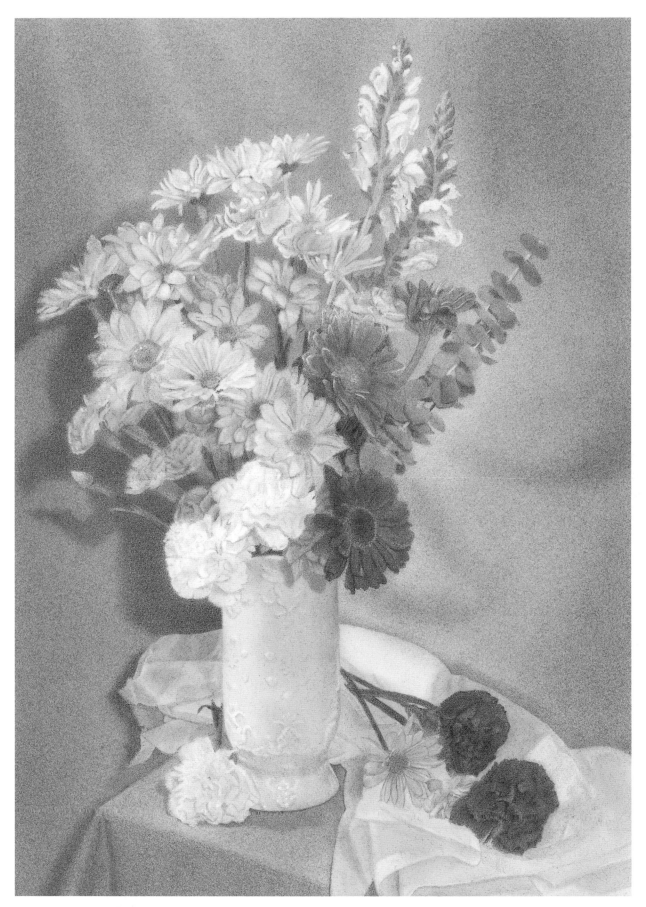

Step 7 Now add the raised pattern to the vase by further smoothing the gradation of value and pulling out the design with a kneaded eraser. Then lightly add shadows beneath the highlights of the raised area. As you proceed, hold your drawing at arm's length to check and adjust values, heightening contrasts by erasing to form lights and penciling in darks until you are satisfied.

PORTRAIT OF A GIRL

The adult human face features universal proportions, and subtle variations of these proportions create a likeness of a particular individual. Imagine a rectangle surrounding a face: The eyes are located about halfway down the center and are positioned about one eye-width apart; the bottoms of the ears line up with the bottom of the nose; and the corners of the relaxed mouth line up vertically with the pupils.

A child's facial proportions are slightly different than an adult's, as they haven't yet "grown into" some of their features. Children's eyes are farther apart and their noses are broader, flatter, and shorter. Their eyebrows usually are centered halfway down the head.

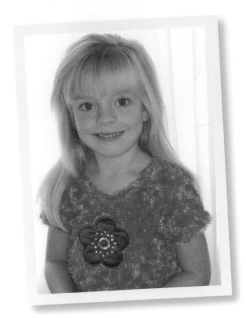

▶ **Paper Choice for Emphasis** Smooth paper will accentuate this child's youthful and flawless complexion, as it will allow the subtle gradations necessary to replicate her skin.

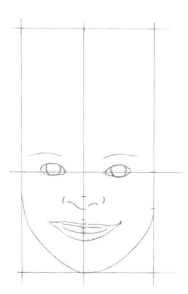

Step 1 Begin by marking the width and height of the face on your paper, and then use these marks to create a rectangular framework for the face. Indicate the position of the major features with dashes, taking care to maintain accurate proportions. Measure the height of the eyes in relation to the rest of the features; then lightly sketch in the eyes and nostrils, and use the relationship of the eyes to the corners of the mouth to sketch the mouth.

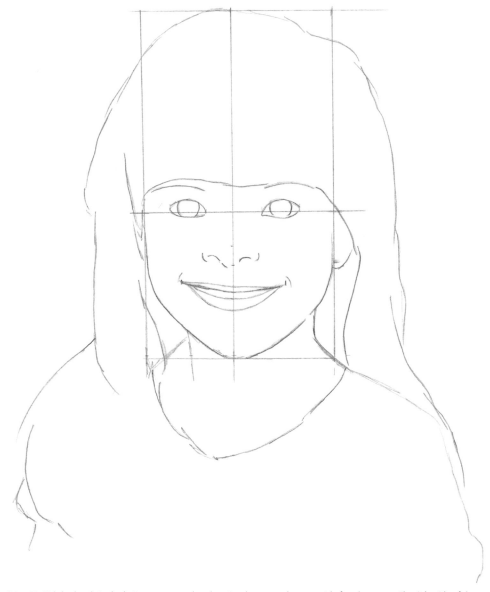

Step 2 Lightly sketch in the hair, sweater, and neck, using the rectangle as a guide for placement. The right side of the neck flows into her jawline near the bottom of the mouth, and the left side flows out midway between her bottom lip and chin. Continue to use comparisons for size and placement of the features.

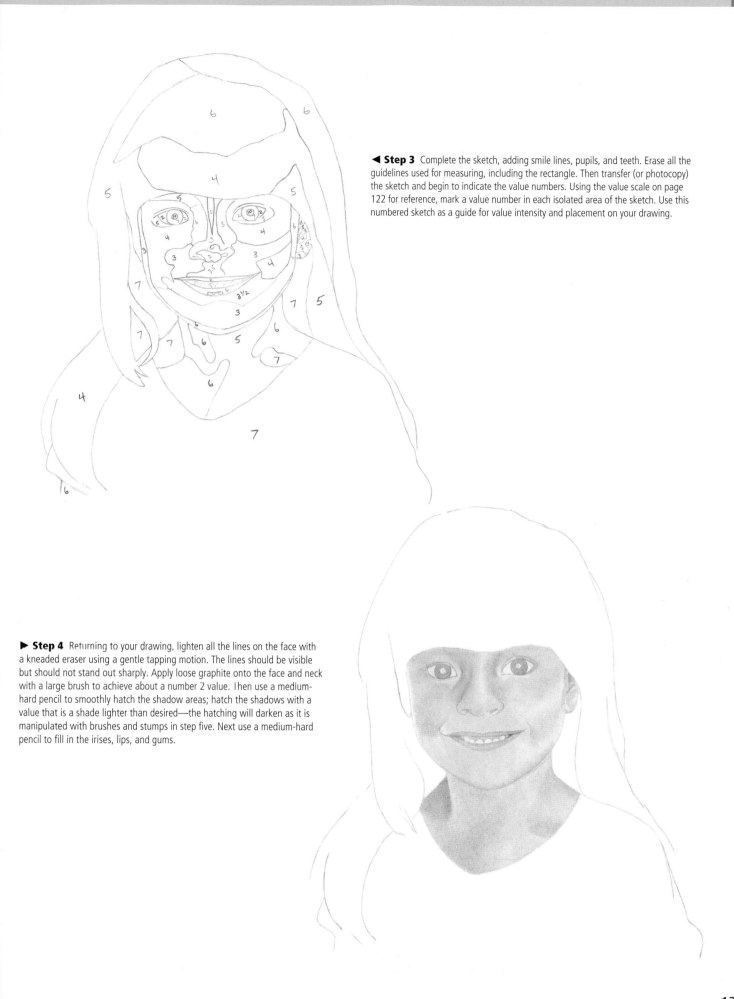

◄ **Step 3** Complete the sketch, adding smile lines, pupils, and teeth. Erase all the guidelines used for measuring, including the rectangle. Then transfer (or photocopy) the sketch and begin to indicate the value numbers. Using the value scale on page 122 for reference, mark a value number in each isolated area of the sketch. Use this numbered sketch as a guide for value intensity and placement on your drawing.

► **Step 4** Returning to your drawing, lighten all the lines on the face with a kneaded eraser using a gentle tapping motion. The lines should be visible but should not stand out sharply. Apply loose graphite onto the face and neck with a large brush to achieve about a number 2 value. Then use a medium-hard pencil to smoothly hatch the shadow areas; hatch the shadows with a value that is a shade lighter than desired—the hatching will darken as it is manipulated with brushes and stumps in step five. Next use a medium-hard pencil to fill in the irises, lips, and gums.

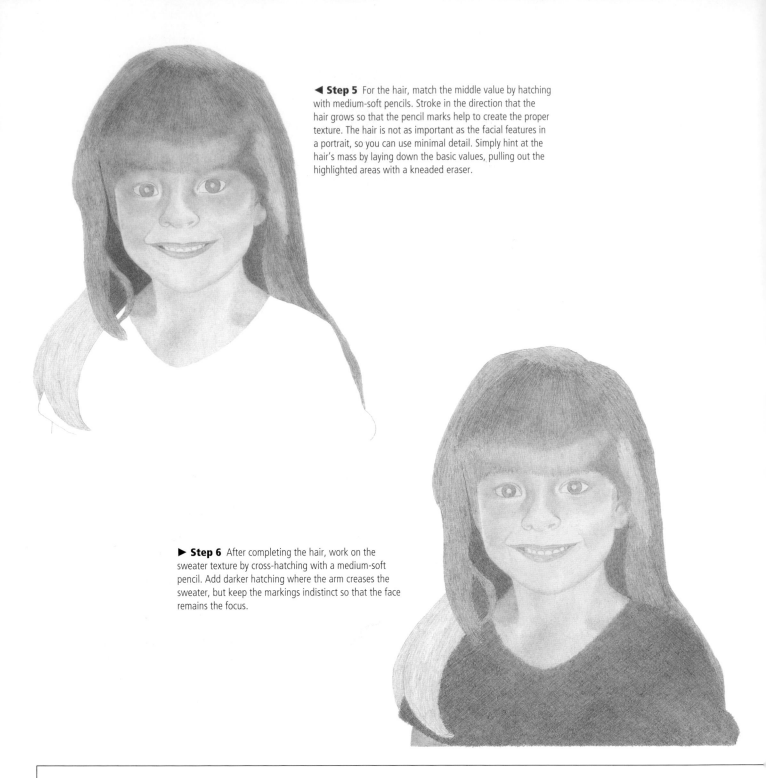

◄ Step 5 For the hair, match the middle value by hatching with medium-soft pencils. Stroke in the direction that the hair grows so that the pencil marks help to create the proper texture. The hair is not as important as the facial features in a portrait, so you can use minimal detail. Simply hint at the hair's mass by laying down the basic values, pulling out the highlighted areas with a kneaded eraser.

► Step 6 After completing the hair, work on the sweater texture by cross-hatching with a medium-soft pencil. Add darker hatching where the arm creases the sweater, but keep the markings indistinct so that the face remains the focus.

Drawing the Eyes

Step 1 Use a medium-soft pencil to outline the iris, pupil, and lids. Then indicate the curvature of the eyebrow and the edge of the nose.

Step 2 The "white" portion of the eye is a number 2 value, so darken the entire area accordingly using a brush and graphite powder.

Step 3 Using a medium-hard pencil, lightly hatch in the shadow areas around the eye, including the upper lid and the top of the cheek.

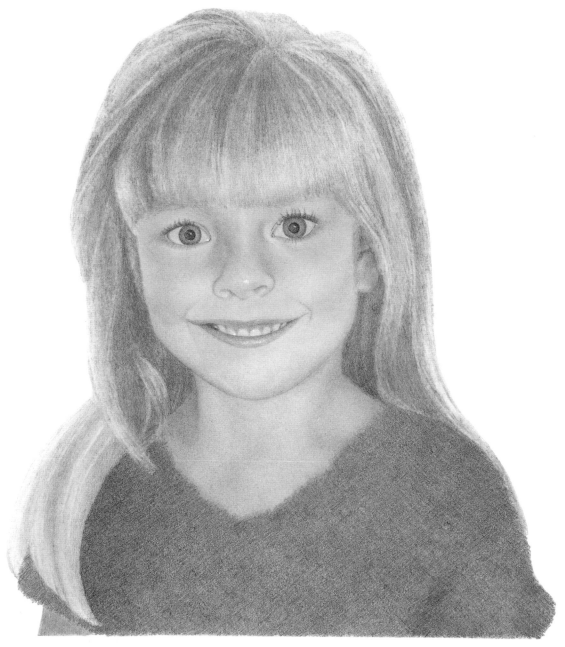

Step 7 Use a brush and a stump to gently rub and stroke the hatching, darkening and smoothing the skin. Graduate the values along the nose and add a highlight on the tip using the sharp point of a battery-powered eraser. Use a medium-soft pencil to add dark details to the eyelids, pupils, irises, nostrils, and corners of the mouth. Then lift out a highlights in the corner of the left eye, on the bottom lip, and on two of the teeth. Finally, smooth the texture of the hair and add thin highlights with a kneaded eraser formed to a point.

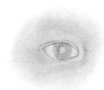

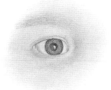

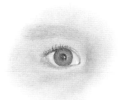

Step 4 Darken the outline of the eye and iris, radiating the strokes outward from the pupil. Then darken the shadows using a brush, loose graphite, and a stump.

Step 5 Outline the iris and fill in the pupil, working around the highlight. Smooth the iris with a stump; then darken the eyebrow and corners of the eye.

Step 6 Use a soft pencil to stroke in the upper eyelashes, followed by the lower lashes with a hard pencil. Pull out highlights in the corner of the eye.

FRUIT & WINE

When using only pencil—essentially a range of grays—incorporating contrasts of texture and value into your drawings is important for creating interest. In this scene, the sharp, crisp highlights on the wine glass, bowl, and pieces of fruit nicely contrast against the soft, velvety fabric background. Also the light values of the pears and grapes are a great complement to the dark background.

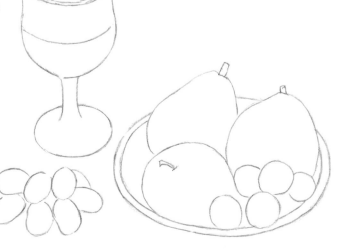

▶ **Choosing Paper** The soft folds of the fabric and sleek surfaces of the fruit's skin call for a smooth watercolor paper.

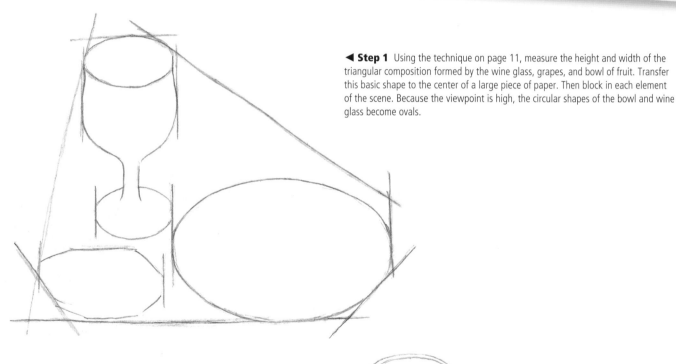

◀ **Step 1** Using the technique on page 11, measure the height and width of the triangular composition formed by the wine glass, grapes, and bowl of fruit. Transfer this basic shape to the center of a large piece of paper. Then block in each element of the scene. Because the viewpoint is high, the circular shapes of the bowl and wine glass become ovals.

▶ **Step 2** Now begin refining the outlines of each element. Indicate the level of the wine in the glass and each grape in the cluster below the glass. Then add the edge of the bowl, and sketch the fruit, taking care to maintain the proportions shown in the reference photo. When everything is in place, erase the initial guidelines.

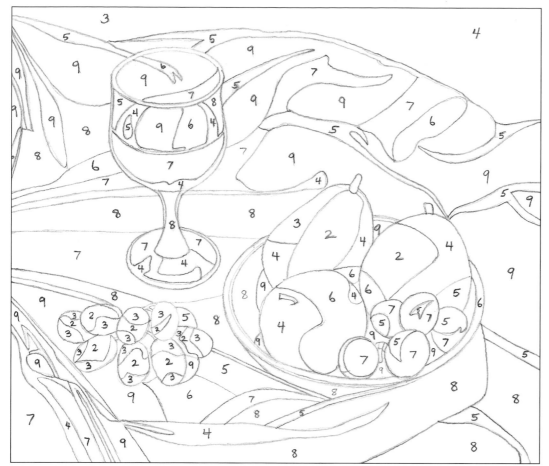

◄ **Step 3** Next draw the upper curve of the cloth, noting how far it is above both the glass and the bowl in the reference. Then draw the wrinkles and folds of the cloth. When you are finished, transfer the drawing onto another sheet of paper (or photocopy the sketch) and assign a value number to each area according to the value scale on page 122. Use this as a guide for value intensity and placement.

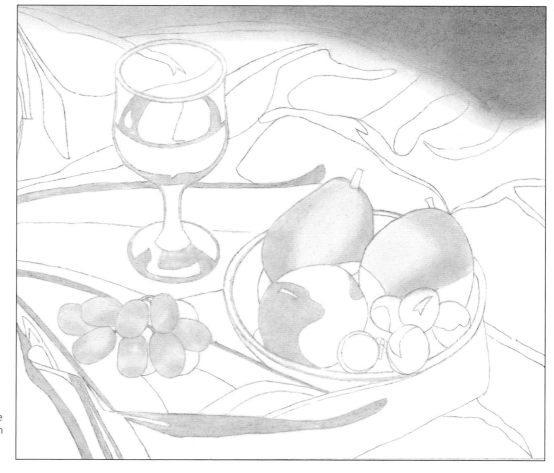

► **Step 4** Prepare a pile of loose graphite and fill in the far wall (at top) using a wide brush. Graduate to a slightly darker value on the right side to add interest to the negative space. Take your strokes down past the top of the fabric to make it appear as though the fabric is in front of the background. Then add a range of medium and light values in the folds, on the fruit, and in the glass using a smaller brush and loose graphite.

Creating a Wine Glass

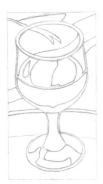

◀ **Step 1** Draw the outline of the glass, and then squint your eyes to see the shapes of the values in it.

▶ **Step 2** Use tight hatching to fill each area with a range of dark and medium values.

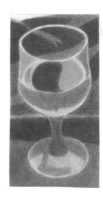

◀ **Step 3** Smooth the separations in value using a small brush. Then begin hatching and smoothing the darkest areas of the wine glass.

▶ **Step 4** Add details using a sharp soft lead for the shadows along the base of the glass and within the stem. Then lift out highlights with a stick eraser, accenting the edges of the glass for a sharp contrast to the dark cloth.

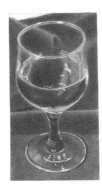

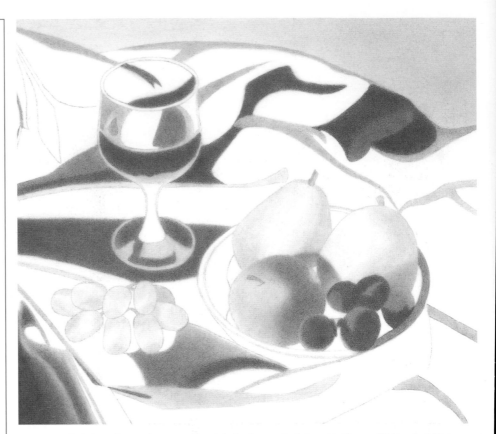

Step 5 Apply darker values to the composition, bringing form to the fruit and further establishing the folded pattern of the fabric. Use medium-hard and soft pencils, depending on the value. Hatch each area, smoothing the hatching with a small brush and repeating the process until the area reaches the desired value.

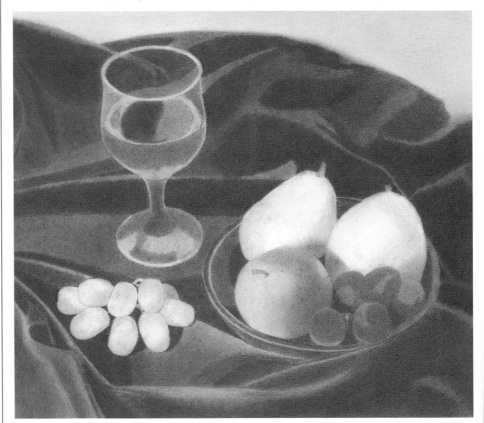

Step 6 To create the very dark values in the surrounding cloth, use sharp, very soft leads for hatching. Follow each layer of hatching with a brush to smooth out the lines, repeating this until you achieve the darkest darks. Because it's possible to lift graphite by brushing it, keep your brush smoothing to a minimum as you approach the final value.

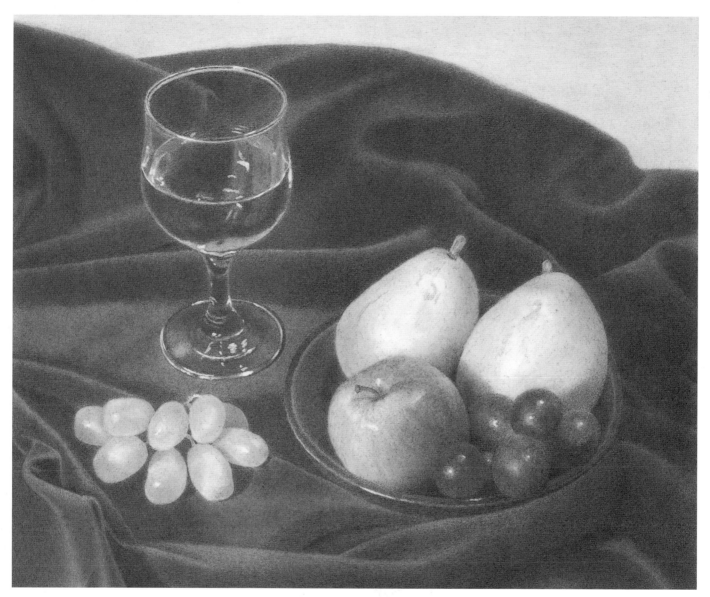

Step 7 In this step, gradually blend the dark areas of the cloth into the highlighted areas of its folds using soft leads and a brush. The dark grapes are similar in value to the bowl, so pay careful attention when separating the grapes' edges from the bowl and from one another. Looking carefully at the shadows that the lighter grapes are casting on one another, apply more graphite to the bodies of the grapes using a small brush. Add a grainy texture to the pears with hard lead followed by light brushing. For the apple, use a kneaded eraser to lift out highlights and a hard lead to add subtle dark stripes. To finish the drawing, create the sharpest contrast possible by pulling out crisp highlights on the fruit, bowl, and wine glass with a battery-powered eraser.

CLOSING WORDS

With each attempt at drawing, you will go a little further and learn a little more. Remember that this journey is not about making perfect drawings: it's about making each drawing you create better than the one before it while having a good time. There are plenty of important ideas in my chapter, but none of them are useful until they are put into practice. I wish you much success in your drawing adventures!

—Ken Goldman

Artists who draw and paint are more fortunate than a sculptor or photographer in that we can move elements around in our composition. We can change their size and shape and place them where we feel they look best to be more harmonious with all the other elements. I hope the various compositional methods presented in my chapter will be of great assistance to you when creating your own dynamic composition.

—William F. Powell

It is with great pleasure that I share my methods of creating texture with pencil. Explore some of your own favorite subjects while employing the techniques that you have been exposed to in my chapter. Have the confidence to experiment with textural qualities, and remember that the most important ingredient is your passion for creating art. In time, you will find your own way to create magic with your pencil.

—Diane Cardaci

As a note of encouragement, I'd like to remind you that a path leading anywhere is best followed one step at a time. This is true of life as well as art! To finish a drawing, you need to work on it step by step; to become accomplished in this medium, you need to create one drawing after another. And to be an artist, simply continue down this path of self-expression—step by step, drawing by drawing. As you travel, don't forget to look back at your earlier drawings every now and then. Your progress will amaze and delight you—looking back to see how far you've come will inspire you to keep drawing and growing artistically. Enjoy the journey!

—Carol Rosinski